HUGH KINGSMILL

HUGH KINGSMILL IN 1948
A year before his death

MICHAEL HOLROYD

HUGH KINGSMILL

A
CRITICAL BIOGRAPHY

WITH AN INTRODUCTION
BY MALCOLM MUGGERIDGE

faber and faber

This edition first published in 2009
by Faber and Faber Ltd
Bloomsbury House, 74–77 Great Russell Street
London WC1B 3DA

Printed by CPI Antony Rowe, Eastbourne

A CIP record for this book is available from the British Library

ISBN 978-0-571-25278-7

TO
WILLIAM GERHARDI

Contents

Introduction

THOSE OF US WHO KNEW HUGH KINGSMILL HAVE CONTINUED
to keep his memory alive among ourselves. It is rare, for instance,
when Hesketh Pearson and I are together, for us not to find
some occasion to mention his name, recall some observation of
his, refer to one or other of his books. But his works are now
out of print, and though most of his brilliant intuitions—for
instance about Matthew Arnold and Dickens—have been sustained by subsequent research, credit is rarely accorded him by
name. More often than not, those who draw on his conclusions,
if they mention him at all, do so disparagingly. How delightful, then, for we who love and revere Kingsmill still, that the
first full-length study of him and his works should be under-
taken, not by one of the diminishing and ageing band of his
intimates, but by a young man, Michael Holroyd, born into
the world Kingsmill was leaving. It was, for me, an intensely
moving experience to read Holroyd's book; the more so because it was mature and perceptive to a degree one would
scarcely have expected in so youthful an author.

When, later, I made Holroyd's acquaintance, this favourable
impression was only confirmed. He seemed to have got the
hang of Kingsmill in an almost miraculous way. Indeed, there
is something miraculous about the whole venture—in Holroyd's having stumbled upon a writer so remote from his generation, and in his immediate awareness of his unique qualities;
in his patient and resolute pursuit of information about Kingsmill and his writings; in the diligence and courage which
enabled him to complete his task, and endure without losing
heart a succession of disappointments over getting the book
published. Now, at last, all is set for its appearance, and I consider it a signal honour to have been asked to undertake this
introduction by way of helping to launch it.

Others of Kingsmill's friends would have been, in many
respects, more appropriate. William Gerhardi knew him longer

than I, and understood certain sides of his character more intimately. Hesketh Pearson was the closest of all of us to Kingsmill, and over a longer period. He collaborated with him in three delightful volumes (*Skye High, This Blessed Plot, Talking of Dick Whittington*), and has a knowledge of the books and writers most interesting to Kingsmill to which I cannot pretend. It was a delight which I can never forget to listen to them, as I so often did, talking about these books and writers, ranging from Frank Harris to William Wordsworth, from *A Gentleman of France* to *Tom Jones*, from Scott to Thackeray, Shakespeare to Dickens, Johnson to Carlyle, Oscar Wilde, Shaw, Conan Doyle, P. G. Wodehouse. One qualification at least I can claim—that I truly loved and revered Kingsmill. He is the only human being I have ever known in whose company I never suffered one moment of boredom : whose solid figure I never saw looming up, and whose voice I never once heard, except with unalloyed happiness. Alas, I have had numerous quarrels, and spoken and written many harsh words. It is a great satisfaction to me now to reflect that, in Kingsmill's case, our relations were free from any taint of anger or resentment; that I never spoke or thought other than affectionately of him. If others criticized him in my presence (and he was open to criticism, of course) I adopted the practice of pointing out that I was too beholden to him to be prepared even to undertake his defence; that whatever he might do or say, however he might conduct himself, the balance of obligation, as far as I was concerned, was so overwhelmingly on my side that I could neither censure him myself nor accept censure from others.

I first met Kingsmill in Manchester in 1929, when I was working there on the *Guardian*. His brother Brian, whom I knew through my wife's family, had often spoken to me about him. So had Louis Wilkinson, the first authentic man-of-letters with whom I was acquainted. Wilkinson had, at that time, a red spade beard, and wore a black hat with a large brim, and seemed to my adolescent eye every inch a writer. He described how once he had come upon Kingsmill unexpectedly, and had seen him gazing somewhat disconsolately at his face in a mirror. The description stuck in my mind. Intimacies cast their shadows before them; they begin in advance of acquaintanceship. This is why the first sight of someone who will be dear to one is never of a stranger. Love originates in a past too remote to be measured, and is projected into a future likewise immeasurable. You take someone's hand, look into their eyes, even in certain cases enfold them in an embrace, before you know, or even think to ask, their name.

Thus, when I saw Kingsmill coming to the barrier at Manchester Central Station I at once knew him, and began talking to him as to an intimate. Thenceforth we went on so talking, on and off, until he died, twenty years later almost to the day. He was a substantial man with a rolling gait, rather like a sailor's. His head was exceptionally large; his hair, already grey, sparse and dishevelled. He never wore a hat. His complexion was ruddy, and he conveyed an impression, even when he was full of troubles, of immense cheerfulness. Happiness glowed in the innermost core of his being, and no outward mist could for long keep its rays from piercing through—a happiness based, not on his circumstances (which were often atrocious), but on an inward serenity, a close and unbreakable relationship with the sublime realities of human life. Kingsmill's complaints were always addressed to the phenomenal world, which he saw as a shadow hiding the real one, like the moon momentarily obscuring the light of the sun in an eclipse. "Poor old mankind," he would sometimes mutter, as he might affectionately about some friend who had run into a lamp-post, or fallen down a man-hole.

His cheerfulness was, I dare say, a certain handicap to him professionally. I have noticed a strong pre-disposition to believe that writers should, like Don Quixote, wear woeful countenances—the more woeful, the higher their earnings. There was little trace of woe in Kingsmill's countenance, and his earnings were correspondingly meagre. A hostile reaction to our laughter was not uncommon when we were together; for instance, on the top of a bus, or walking along the Strand. People did not like it. There is something about laughter which calls in question the whole edifice of established authority and, equally, established opposition to it.* As Kingsmill would put it, laughter, on behalf of the imagination, challenges the will. A man described to me once how he was thrown out of a brothel in Marseilles because he could not forbear laughing at a pornographic film which was being shown there to stimulate business. One sees the point. Pornography, like power, is only

* A favourite quotation of Kingsmill's illustrating the point was from *King John*:

"that idiot, laughter . . .
a passion hateful to my purposes."

effective as long as it is seriously regarded. Those who laugh
are inimical to order and propriety, in brothels as in churches
and ministries.

Kingsmill's laughter was highly characteristic. It came from
within and spread outwards. Some notion would start him
off, and, as he developed and expanded its absurdity, so his
laughter would wax correspondingly. I remember once, when
he and Pearson and I were lunching together at the Horseshoe
in Tottenham Court Road, we started speculating about the
weekly visits which Samuel Butler and his friend Festing Jones
used to pay severally to a French lady residing in Handel
Street. As Kingsmill explored the theme—which of them went
first? What was Madame's verdict on their relative perform-
ances? Did Butler take with him a sponge-bag containing his
kit? And so on—our laughter rose. Finally, we decided to go
to Handel Street, where we identified the house. Standing in
front of it, Kingsmill produced such a hilarious picture of these
two bearded sentimental homosexuals on their curious errand
that we were reduced to hanging helplessly on to lamp-posts
to contain our mirth, to the astonishment, and sometimes
irritation, of occasional passers-by. Even now, if ever I pass
by Handel Street, the memory of the scene returns, and makes
me want to laugh again.

The idea in getting Kingsmill to Manchester was to try and
arrange some book reviewing for him on the *Guardian*. To
this end I took him along to the office. We leader-writers
worked in what was known as the Corridor; a place of
shadows, doubtless haunted, among others, by the tortured
ghost of C. E. Montague. I introduced Kingsmill to the literary
editor, Alan Monkhouse, but could see from the beginning
that the interview was not going well. The sensitive, talented,
but somehow forlorn Monkhouse shrank from him, as, to my
amazement, people often did. It was sometimes suggested that
his manners were not of the best. In the sense that he never
could feign interest in anyone or anything which he did not
feel, there may have been an element of plausibility in this.
His own thoughts and speculations were so absorbing that he
was often oblivious to his surroundings, and might finish off
a plate of cakes, or monopolize the fireside, without knowing
what he was doing. This was liable to annoy a certain type of
person, as was Kingsmill's relentless honesty of mind, called
tactlessness by those who feared and shunned it.

In any case, the *Guardian,* and the already creaking, groan-

ing, derelict liberalism it represented, had no place for him, or
he for it. On our way home in the evening we looked over the
next day's leaders, noticing, with much hilarity, one which
began : "One is sometimes tempted to believe that the Greeks
do not want a stable government," and went on to express the
hope that "moderate men of all shades of opinion" would rally
round someone or other. Thenceforth, we often spoke of
"moderate men of all shades of opinion."

It is difficult to convey the delight, the variety, the sparkle
and the immense verve of Kingsmill's talk. Merely quoting
observations he made will not serve. They have to be fitted into
the theme out of which they emerged, into the wealth of
illustration used to embellish them, into the flow of quotations
and references of which he had so seemingly inexhaustible a
store. For his numerous anthologies he practically never needed
to look anything up. It was all in his head, and he could
prepare one (as I have known him do) in a matter of ten days,
and without reference to any library other than his own few
shelves of books. To me, his talk was, and remains, one of
the greatest pleasures I have ever experienced. It was not only
that he talked himself; he stimulated talk in others. No one
was ever less oracular than he, or more ready to listen and be
amused. Holroyd says that I was his disciple, and this is true;
except that, by his very nature, Kingsmill never could have a
disciple. He made one feel mentally alive as no one else I have
ever met did. He raised one up to his own level. To this day
there is not one book I spoke with Kingsmill about whose
pages do not still glow with his touch. Once, when we were
in the British Museum (a place we both loathed, and which
I have never entered since his death), we overheard one of
the uniformed attendants ask another where so-and-so was.
"He's in the Illuminated," was the reply. Kingsmill took me
into the Illuminated. In a sane world he would have been a
professor; but then, in a world as sane as that, there would be
no need for professors. The teachers I had at school and Cambridge were so derisory as to make no impact whatsoever. I
forgot them at once and everything they taught. It was from
Kingsmill I learnt that the pursuit of understanding is so en-
thralling that all others seem, by comparison, lustreless; that,
as he so often quoted, all the world's in a grain of sand, and
ecstacy lies in holding it up to catch the light.

Kingsmill's visit to Manchester was entirely dedicated to
talk. He had lately come out of hospital, where he underwent

some minor operation, and dilated upon how happy he had been, looked after by amiable nurses, and secure against any demands, personal or monetary, from the outside world. He liked whatever shut him off from the business and noise of life, and provided a lull for him to meditate and take his ease. Thus, nothing pleased him more than to settle into a first-class railway carriage with a long journey before him. This indulgence was permissible as long as he could procure a free pass from the travel agency, founded by his father, Sir Henry Lunn. When that got into difficulties, his railway travelling was correspondingly curtailed. Even his time in captivity in the 1914-18 war, in retrospect, had a pleasant glow. He used to say that it would have been perfect if he could have drawn on it from time to time as required, instead of having to take it in a lump sum.

While he was with me in Manchester, Kingsmill had some notion that Pearson, then a professional actor, would pass through Salford on his way back to London from Newcastle-upon-Tyne, where he had been appearing. We spent an agreeable Sunday morning walking up and down the platform of Salford Station; not among the world's beauty-spots, but to me, then, in the new enchantment of Kingsmill's company, delectable enough. Pearson, I need scarcely say, did not appear. Nor, as I subsequently learnt from him, was there any particular reason to suppose that he would. Kingsmill's congenital impracticability derived from an engrained habit of entertaining the, in his eyes eminently reasonable, assumption that whatever he thought desirable was bound to happen. Nor did he ever cease to be surprised and hurt when this assumption proved unfounded. Even so, in retrospect I see our fruitless vigil on Salford Station as a portent of the many happy hours that the three of us were to pass together.

The next time I saw Kingsmill was in Hastings, where he was living in a wooden house called "The Old Mill", on a hill overlooking the town and the sea. He had returned to England from a sojourn in Thonon-les-Bains to, as he said, face his creditors. Having taken this honourable and courageous action, he went on, it was preposterous to expect him to carry matters further and pay them. He had an abiding affection for Hastings which lasted to the end of his life, and which I came to share. His father, in the mysterious operation of his enterprises, had acquired control of the Albany Hotel there. When he was young, Kingsmill lived in it, relatively free from financial and other cares. It was, perhaps, the memory of these youthful times which endeared the place to him. The Albany was an old-fashioned establishment, patronized by an elderly and often decrepit clientèle. Kingsmill described them once, with some acerbity, as excrement living on increment. In the 1939-45 war it was first evacuated, and then received a direct hit which has totally obliterated it.

It was in the five years before 1939 that I saw most of Kingsmill. He was still living in Hastings, but in a larger, more solid house in Laton Road, and I was living in the village of Whatlington some seven miles away. We met frequently; Pearson came often to stay with one or other of us, or in the George at Battle. Brian Lunn, Kingsmill's younger brother, was also residing in Hastings with his two children, in a house built, and formerly occupied, by a monumental mason. Half-finished tombstones lay about the garden, and the interior arrangements had a vaguely funereal aspect. The lady who conducted the household was named Mrs. Pitcher; the widow of a petty officer in the navy, sharp tongued and somewhat bizarre in appearance, in the style of a pantomime dame, but kind-hearted and capable. Brian with his wide expanse of rubicund face, and of equally rubicund bald pate, was a familiar figure in Hastings, as, wearing the late Petty Officer Pitcher's white shorts, he made his way to the sea in all weathers for a morning bathe. He provided the subject for Kingsmill's novel, *The Fall,* by, on one occasion, falling on his head from the top of a London bus. The subsequent temporary derangements of his wits suggested to Kingsmill another Fall; this time from the fantasy of the will and into the reality of the imagination, instead of the other way round, as in the Garden of Eden. This finer shade of significance in Brian's accident was momentarily eclipsed when we visited him together in hospital. Two male attendants, who were standing by in case of violence, took the opportunity to withdraw, and Kingsmill and I looked at one another with an anxious eye across Brian's—as we hoped—recumbent body.

It seems to me now, looking back, that those summers, before the hideous chain of events from August 1939, were full of sunshine. I saw Kingsmill most days, or had long telephone conversations with him. Either I would bicycle into Hastings, or he came out to me, taking the bus to Battle, and walking the last mile or so to Whatlington. Usually I would meet him along the way, delighted when his solid figure loomed up, and he

began to wave, and shout his cheerful greeting—"Hullo! old
man! Hullo!" His cheerfulness, which made some shudder
like an east wind, arose out of his basic attitude to life. He
saw the imagination and the will locked in interminable conflict. The imagination generated love, serenity, literature, faith,
laughter, understanding; the will, appetite, in the individual
for sensual satisfactions and in the collectivity for power. Kingsmill came to live so exclusively in the imagination that the
pursuit of power, and all its ancillary imbecilities—on a broad
front, ranging from Hitler to D. H. Lawrence, and taking in all
the various contemporary utopians, or dawnists, as he used to
call them—filled him with a kind of derisory wonder. This
was one of the reasons his company was so pleasurable. He had
no part in the age's grisly buffooneries. I asked him once what
he did when, in the first world war, he found himself among
the enemy. "I tried to convince them that my intentions
were pacific," he replied. In an age of collectivism, all collective remedies and hopes seemed to him intrinsically fal-
lacious. As he put it in his introduction to *The Poisoned
Crown*:

> "What is divine in man is elusive and impalpable, and
> he is easily tempted to embody it in a collective form—
> a church, a country, a social system, a leader—so that
> he may realize it with less effort and serve it with more
> profit. Yet, as even Lincoln proved, the attempt to ex-
> ternalize the kingdom of heaven in a temporal shape must
> end in disaster. It cannot be created by charters or
> constitutions, nor established by arms. Those who set out
> for it alone will reach it together and those who seek it
> in company will perish by themselves."

Have any words more truly and exactly expressed the basic
fallacy of the various earthly paradises offered to mankind
in our time, with consequence so bloody and so ruinous? The
clarity of Kingsmill's vision, and the opposition he so amusingly
and good-naturedly, but confidently, offered to prevailing
trends, may have cost him the moderate popular success he
humanly craved, but it also brought him an inward happiness
and serenity which few of his contemporaries were capable
of even understanding, still less experiencing. However sour
or apocalyptic one's mood, with him laughter was always

lurking round the corner; above the dark clouds there was the azure sky—that sense which never can quite desert us, and which abode with Kingsmill more than with most, of the sheer blessedness of being alive. Once we stood looking down on old Hastings on a still autumn evening. From each separate chimney there came a wreath of smoke; like souls, he said, climbing up into the sky.

In the worst days of the London blitz, Kingsmill was staying in Pearson's flat in St. John's Wood, and spent a lot of time listening to gramophone records of Beethoven's slow movements, to which he was greatly addicted. Pearson and his wife had moved to be near us at Whatlington, and Kingsmill's only companion was a certain Aunty Bee, who had also, by marriage, a Roumanian name which nobody seemed to know, a lady of a somewhat unequal temper and no great physical beauty, who none-the-less got along famously with Kingsmill. This oddly assorted couple took little account of the mighty deluge of bombs, which, in Kingsmill's eyes, were just another example of the will's insanity. They made endless cups of tea, and Kingsmill addressed the running commentary on life which so delighted his friends, in their absence, to Aunty Bee. What she made of it, if anything, has never been discovered, but she always spoke appreciatively of the time she spent with Kingsmill. Coming from Aunty Bee, who was normally of a decidedly critical temper, this was an outstanding tribute to the charm of his company.

In the first years of the war Kingsmill had various teaching jobs, which he greatly enjoyed; for the work itself, and above all, for the relative easing of his financial troubles that they provided. Money worries were his torment, and certainly hastened his end. Though he was very abstemious himself, and lived modestly enough with his wife and three children, he never could seem to earn enough money to meet his expenses. There was a constant delivery of unpaid bills, solicitors' letters and other intimations of penury, at his house, to the point that he hated and dreaded the post, and delighted in public holidays when none came. How often he would set off to London from Hastings under the urgent necessity to lay hands on some money, and with no clear idea how to do it! On one of these occasions, seeing no other recourse, he decided to approach Shaw. He found him in his sitting-room at Whitehall Court, sitting bolt upright in a chair, and looking, as Kingsmill put it, as though made of cotton-wool. On such occasions, out of shyness and distaste, Kingsmill was liable to be brutally blunt, and confine himself simply to saying in an angry tone of voice that he was in need of money. Shaw heard him out and, without a word, reached for his cheque-book, and wrote a cheque for ten pounds. Kingsmill afterwards considered that he should have stood out for fifteen pounds. It was, in any case, a final settlement for whatever unease Shaw felt at Kingsmill's straightened circumstances compared with his own affluence. I should add that, as far as his friends were concerned, if money passed from them to him, it was invariably on their initiative, and involved no initial embarrassment or subsequent pain.

Kingsmill's inability to cope with his money requirements was part of an innate unworldliness which was not, as is so often the case, in any way affected. He never could quite reconcile himself to being a resident on earth, but rather felt himself to be a visitor, who continually marvelled at the strange sights it offered and the truly extraordinary behaviour of the natives. He would lurch against things and against people, physically and metaphorically, because his eyes and heart were set on another scene, of which his actual circumstances were but a poor image. This clumsiness, of behaviour and of disposition, was an integral part of his whole character and attitude of mind, and as such, to his intimates, most touching and loveable. He was like an actor who, unaccountably, had learnt the lines of another play than the one that was being performed, and so stumbled against the unfamiliar scenery, and spoke a part of which the prompter had no knowledge, and made unsuitable exits and entrances.

As far as his finances were concerned, matters were made worse because, up to the age of forty, he had been accustomed to a condition of relatively effortless affluence. His father took him, along with his two brothers, into the family tourist business, and as long as that throve, Kingsmill was assured of an adequate income without undue inroads upon his time and inclination. He never could quite see why or how this agreeable arrangement should have come to an end, and was inclined, in moments of irritation with his money worries, to suppose that he had been deliberately excluded from the Lunn business. Actually the business itself, for a variety of reasons, had ceased to thrive) and there was no superflux (a word Kingsmill particularly liked), as used by King Lear when he belatedly discovered the existence of the poor :

"Take physic, pomp;
Expose thyself to feel what wretches feel,
That thou mayst shake the superflux to them.
And show the heavens more just")

to be shaken in his direction. It is true that the break-up of
Kingsmill's first marriage coincided with his ejection from the
business. Even so, his matrimonial troubles only, at worst,
hastened what would sooner or later have become inevitable
anyway.

So many scenes and conversations with Kingsmill come to
mind, but I must forbear for fear of intruding unduly upon
Holroyd's excellent book. In the latter years of the war Kingsmill worked on *Punch*, and I visited him occasionally in the
Bouverie Street office. The first time, I remember, a sort of
chill struck me; no doubt a premonition that I was going to be
entombed there myself for five years. How often, during that
five years, I regretted his absence as I struggled unavailingly
with the hopeless task of making the English laugh! A more
cheerful meeting-place was the office of the *New English
Review*, where the amiable Miss Cast (also now, alas, dead)
ministered valiantly and lovingly to Kingsmill's vagrant clerical
needs during the time that he was literary editor, and whence
he took review copies of books to sell to our friend and bene-
factor, Mr. Gaston, whose premises were then situated in the
Strand. It was a transaction for which Kingsmill ever had the
greatest possible respect and esteem.

His appearance was always so robust that it was difficult
to believe that his health was failing. Yet there were signs. He
grew tired easily, and once, when some lucrative but tedious
writing assignment was proposed to him, he burst out that little
time remained, and he could ill spare any of it for such work.
I noticed that, as he said this, his eyes filled with tears. After
his first spell in hospital he stayed with me in Regent's Park,
where I was then living. He seemed to recover, and we spent
many happy hours in the Park, which Kingsmill always loved
because, he said, it was a gentle and restrained image of nature,
which could be so turbulent and so cruel. The second time he
went into hospital in Brighton was the end. Pearson and I
visited him. We went separately so as to tire him less and make
the visits more. The last time I saw him he was very weak, and
held my hand—an unusual thing for him, who was, by temperament, undemonstrative. He had, he said, some good news

to impart; something wonderful which had come to him about our human situation. He never did manage to get it out, but none-the-less, unspoken, it has often comforted me. As I get older, and approach my own end, it even seems that I know what he had to communicate with ever greater precision and certainty. His sense of humour remained unimpaired. One of the nurses, he told me, had remarked to the doctor that he was holding on to life like grim death. He was in a public ward, and as usual had delighted and fascinated his fellow-patients. I used to ring up the hospital in anguish every morning for news of him. The last time, owing to some telephonic accident, I intruded upon two strange voices. Though I could not distinguish what they were saying, they seemed to be full of a malice and foreboding which chilled my blood. When I got through to the hospital I heard that Kingsmill was dead.

Before writing this introduction, I re-read all Kingsmill's works, some of them for the fourth and fifth time. I leave their analysis to Holroyd's fresher mind, and content myself with saying that I enjoyed and admired them more than ever; that *The Progress of a Biographer* seemed to me a distillation of Kingsmill's unique wisdom; *The Poisoned Crown* to say all anyone ever need know about the cruelties and buffooneries of power; the *Frank Harris* to be a biographical masterpiece on a par with Johnson's *Life of Savage*, and *The High Hill of the Muses* to contain what is most wonderful in the abundant and diverse treasures of our language and literature. I keep it by my bedside always. If Holroyd's book serves to renew interest in these works, to the point that some of them are made available again, he will have done a public service, besides delighting all Kingsmill's friends and admirers.

MALCOLM MUGGERIDGE

1

Background

ONE FRIDAY, EARLY IN THE YEAR 1880, A PARTY OF EXCITED tourists cruising in the Mediterranean, stepped ashore at Cairo to witness the antics of a band of howling and dancing Dervishes. Returning to their ship after the performance was over, two members of the party were seen to detach themselves from the others and, appearing to become engaged in a passionately earnest discussion, it was thought advisable not to interrupt them. The older of the two, a Presbyterian missionary from India, was entreating his twenty year old companion, the son of a Midland grocer, to give his life to Indian missionary work. The young man listened eagerly, but when the missionary had exhausted himself of all his eloquence, still remained uncertain. "For some time," wrote Sir Henry Lunn over fifty years later, "I put the idea to one side, but this conversation afterwards changed the whole direction of my life."

The direction of his life was often to undergo such changes. Possessing an energetic and romantic temperament, he was pulled at one time or another by the attractions of a life devoted to Wesleyan Methodism, to commercial interests; to the pleasures of society and to a career in radical politics, and he contrived ingeniously to merge all these pursuits together so far as they could be considered financially advantageous without endangering the sanctity of his conscience. Within the limits imposed by an active life in groceries, his father found time to practise as a Methodist lay preacher, and had married an intensely religious young woman to whom he had become engaged when she was only fifteen and he eighteen.

21

Henry Simpson Lunn was born on July 30th, 1859, in the small town of Horncastle in Lincolnshire. There was little social activity in the neighbourhood and the boy's early life was uneventful. But even while still a schoolboy he displayed those curiously diversified talents which were to characterize his later years. In the holidays he found relaxation in attending the regular meetings of the Mutual Improvement Society; while during term at Horncastle grammar school he grew industrious on his own account. Like many schoolboys he kept mice as pets. But what remains with most children as a passing hobby, he quickly developed into a thriving and lucrative "mouse farm", the produce of which he judiciously advertised in *The Exchange and Mart*; and soon he was conducting a brisk business whereby he successfully kept replenished his pocket money. Suitably impressed, his father took him into his shop. A few years later his son was to return the compliment with interest.

Henry Lunn's first major financial venture was started at the age of seventeen. That year, 1877, it so happened that the first Wimbledon tournament took place, and to coincide with this event he sent out a circular offering to supply prospective players with lawn tennis sets, which he knew that he could obtain wholesale and sell to the public at a very reasonable profit. Business exceeded the wildest dreams of avarice, but the young man's energy remained unabated. Next, with the active co-operation of the All England Lawn Tennis Club, he published a booklet on lawn tennis, which also contained the rules of the game. It sold well, and the following year he patented an ingenious invention, consisting of a pair of scoring dials fixed on to the racket, just below the gut. News of this gadget spread fast reaching the Prince of Wales and the Duke of Edinburgh, and soon Henry Lunn could proudly name them both among his rapidly increasing number of customers. By now there was no looking back. A new scoring device, not his own, was exploited exclusively to his own profit; further tasteful improvements were effected, such as the printing of business notepaper displaying the Wales crest and motto *"Ich dien"*; from the original few pounds the business expanded and flourished a thousandfold.

The conscience of the rich is a source of wonder to the ordinary man, yet in this case it was not entirely illogical that Henry Lunn should feel troubled by his success. Such an obvious flair for making money was growing acutely embarrassing to the young Wesleyan professing an uncompromising belief in the Catholic principle of poverty as one of the great Christian virtues. After a vivid dream depicting himself stranded in a condition of godless prosperity, he approached his father and sounded him out as to whether he would like to diversify his activities in grocery with an interest in lawn tennis. The response being favourable, he made him the junior partner in the business which he had created, taking a thousand pounds out of it so that he could pay for a course at Dublin University in arts, medicine and divinity, in preparation for missionary work in India.

After attending Headingly College, Leeds, a Methodist Wesleyan training college, for a full two years, he went up to Trinity College, Dublin in October 1883. University life, with its air of social prestige and political opportunity appealed naturally to Henry Lunn. But here, too, there lurked danger. During 1886 he was invited as a successful member of the Contemporary Club to go to England and make speeches shortly before the general election assuring the English voters that Home Rule would not mean the persecution of Irish Protestants by their Catholic fellow-countrymen. He promptly accepted the invitation and once in London was informed that Parnell wished him to take a seat as a Home Rule Member of Parliament. There is no doubt that he was a born politician and that life at Westminster would have suited his nature perfectly. But remembering his dream and the advice of the Presbyterian missionary in Cairo, he resisted this temptation to be diverted from God's work and returned to Dublin where he became instead president of the University Temperance Society.

It was while studying in Dublin that he met his wife. Ethel Moore, the eldest daughter of Prebendary Moore, Rector of Middleton and headmaster of Middleton College in County Cork, had been educated in Germany. A quiet, reserved girl, she possessed a strong and patient will coupled with a love of the picturesque, which hinted at a disquieting imagination kept sternly under control. Resolved to lead a life in the service of others she had gone to Dublin to become a nurse at the Adelaide, which Henry Lunn was attending as a medical student. And there she had fallen in love with him. It is not difficult to guage the nature of his appeal to her. For although their temperaments were altogether dissimilar, he must have seemed to represent all that was finest and most idealistic among mere mortals. For was not this man, so eloquent and enthusiastic, and still only in his twenties, forsaking rich worldly rewards in the true and selfless service of God as he sailed out to the mysterious and unknown East? His example captivated her, appealing as it did to both sides of her nature. And he, supported by her faith and admiration, found new strength in resisting the various temptations which lay in the way of what he had to do. They were married on July 12th, 1887, and three months later set out together for Madras.

"Where the voice of duty calls you," Henry Lunn's mother had told him, "there I wish you to go, to be poured out in the Master's service." The voice of duty had triumphed; he had followed its call. But his life's work for which he had been preparing himself for so long and in pursuing which he had sacrificed so much, ended more quickly than anyone could have anticipated. Altogether, he was poured out in the Master's service one year and four days. For although robust in appearance, his constitution was badly effected by the Indian climate. More time was spent in recovering from bouts of fever than attending the important meetings and congresses, and it was soon apparent that they would have to return to England.

Naturally this was a disappointing set-back for Henry Lunn, but for his wife it was something more; it was disillusion. She had set her heart on a life of steady martyrdom in the out-posts of the world, and now this was to be denied her. Back in Ireland she had held a clear unclouded vision of what a missionary's life should be. Had not the prophets of old wandered from land to far off land as the spirit moved them, regardless of riches and of the elements in their search for God and their burning desire to spread His Word? So, too, would they pitch their tent wherever they were needed, he ministering the Gospel to the dusky natives, while she instructed their wives and pretty children. Reality contrasted strongly with this visionary picture. She found missionaries taking it easy on the verandas of their fine bungalows, lolling in deck chairs waited on by obsequious servants who brought them cool drinks in the heat of the day, and generally enjoying a life organized with all the casual comforts of an occupying army of cavalry officers. Well, she would certainly have something to say about it all when she returned to England.

For some after they came back, Henry Lunn tried vainly to live up to his wife's lofty ideals. Under her influence he campaigned vigorously against the luxurious life led by the Methodist missionaries in India, and after a heated and confused debate at the Wesleyan Methodist Conference, he was assigned to an obscure circuit. The egocentricity of the selfless is of a peculiarly irritating type, with its divine assumption that others should be as impractical as themselves. It was now that the fundamental difference between husband and wife made itself apparent. Within a short time Henry Lunn was collaborating with the journalist W. T. Stead, who had just started his *Review of Reviews*, and a year later he founded a review of his own, based on Stead's and called *A Review of the Churches*. The policy of this paper was to promote Christian unity, and it was to attend a conference on this subject that he went to Grindelwald in 1892. Many leading Nonconformist divines also attended, and Henry Lunn made all the travel arrangements for them. It was not long after this that he established himself at the head of a prosperous but fluctuating travel business. His public service was recognized by a knighthood in 1910, and by several other honours later in his life.

And so his wife's disillusion was complete. The missionary she had married had metamorphosed into a tourist agent, the fiery idealist so supremely qualified to preach sermons to the primitive multitudes of the East had grown into a businessman, accredited by the South Eastern Railway to sell tickets to the *hoi polloi*. It was best, of course, to forget such details, to make sure that they were never mentioned in front of the children. In this, as in other matters, she remained stoical, to the point of apparent cynicism.

By this time four children had been born, three sons and one daughter. The eldest son, Arnold Henry Moore Lunn, was born out in India on April 18th, 1888. Like his father he suffered acutely from fever, and when only a few months old was for some time actually at the point of death. Although less gifted than his two younger brothers, Arnold was to achieve a renown far in excess of either of them. Even at Harrow, where his failure to qualify as a "Blood" made him feel miserably inferior, he rose to become a monitor and gravitated naturally to a position as head of his house. The fitful and intermittent non-conformity of these early years grew weaker at Balliol College, Oxford, where he discovered that his status as secretary to the Union and editor of *The Isis* was hardly less exalted than that of a Harrovian on the edge of the cricket eleven. And all the fire of rebellion was finally extinguished when the author of *The Harrovians,* that spirited attack upon the worship of games, made his mark at the head of the skiing athletocracy in Switzerland. Ski-ing had eclipsed Harrow football; and Arnold's youthful sense of inferiority was annihilated.

The years which followed brought him added fame. He was elected as president of the Ski Club of Great Britain, became a prolific author and celebrated Catholic apologist, was awarded various honours by France, Spain and Switzerland,

and in 1952, as the fitting tribute to an energetic career, he was created a knight. In 1932 when the tourist business had fallen upon hard times he took over Sir Henry Lunn's position as chairman of Alpine Sports Limited, writing to his father that his one prayer was that he might somehow succeed in securing for him and his mother, "a quiet and peaceful old age in return for all the affection which you have both lavished on me throughout my life."

Sir Henry Lunn's two other sons remained less dutiful in their sentiments. Hugh Kingsmill Lunn was born at 46 Torrington Square, in London on November 21st, 1889. Under the pen name of Hugh Kingsmill he wrote biographies, literary criticism, novels, short stories, parodies and travel books, and edited many anthologies. Possibly this versatility did little to assist his literary reputation. In any event, despite the opinion of several critics that by the time of his death at the age of fifty-nine he was on the point of receiving the kudos which was his due, the fact remains that his writings were generally unrecognized during his life-time, and are widely ignored today.

The youngest of the three sons, Brian Holdsworth Lunn, was born in London on November 30th, 1893. A King's scholar and day-boy at Westminster, he was elected to an exhibition at Christ Church, Oxford, in July 1912. The war interrupted his university career, and he was eventually posted as a second lieutenant in the Black Watch to Mesopotamia. From here, due to a number of causes including the effects of the sun, he was invalided out shortly before the end of the war as mentally ill. In his remarkable autobiography, *Switchback,* he has given an account of his extraordinary hallucinations and rapidly succeeding fits of wild exhilaration and despondency, which for sustained and controlled humour, pathos and sensitive detachment has seldom been equalled in autobiographical literature.

Although in many respects a brilliant man, his eccentricity often overcame his brilliance. Unlike his father he did not hold

a strong enough grasp upon everyday reality. Whereas Sir
Henry Lunn could patent inventions and turn them to his own
considerable profit, Brian Lunn's inventions, though duly
patented, seldom worked. On one occasion, watched closely
by William Gerhardi with whom he was then collaborating on
an imaginary history of mankind, *The Memoirs of Satan*, and
who was himself secretly aspiring to become the inventor of a
new form of toothbrush, he tried out a pair of wooden water
wings which he had recently designed. These were attached
with some difficulty to his body by a series of rubber bands,
but once in the water they failed to operate as planned, and
impeded his movements so completely that he could do nothing
but float slowly and helplessly along the full length of the
pool.

Even long after his mental illness, Brian Lunn was subject
to periods of the deepest melancholy which he seemed powerless to resist. When his wife left him later in his life, he was so
dejected that he felt a momentary urge to end it all. Being by
the sea at the time the most ready and convenient means was
obvious. The only objection which he could see to this was the
unpleasantness of getting wet, and this he partly offset by
borrowing a mackintosh from a passing stranger. Fully
equipped, he set out across the beach and entered the sea.
Fortunately, knowing nothing of the peculiar behaviour of
the tides, he had not realized that the shallow water extended
for over a mile off land. A lonely but resolute figure, growing
smaller in the distance, he continued paddling out, while the
level of the water still obstinately refused to rise above his
ankles, until at last, weary and dispirited, he was forced to
abandon the attempt and turn back.

These anecdotes do not appear in *Switchback*, but there
are several included in the book which testify to Brian Lunn's
prevailing sense of inferiority and his dislike of exclusion from
the company of others. This fear of being left an outcast may
have weakened the springs of an original talent, further debili-
tated by his streak of extravagant eccentricity.

Very different from Brian Lunn was his sister, Eileen, born on February 28th, 1897. From the first she worshipped her mother, and during the little services which her father gave all his children on Sunday evenings, she listened enraptured as he spoke to them on the facts of Christian life; and when it was all over and the boys had escaped outside, she would climb up on Sir Henry's knees and earnestly beseech him for a further sermon especially for herself.

It is hardly surprising that both her parents were soon wondering mightily at the young girl's zeal. The Lord had blessed their union with a rare spirit, and determined that such great promise of fruitfulness should not be allowed to wither, they consulted the Bishop of Stepney regarding a suitable establishment of education. As a result of their deliberations, Eileen was sent to a Sisterhood school, St. Mary's, Wantage. It was their wish that their daughter's years here would prepare her for a life of usefulness, and when in company with a school friend she founded a Missionary Study Circle, it seemed as if all their hopes were to be realized.

Better still was to follow. On December 11th, 1916, she was called to the service of God, and, in one of her girl friend's words, "became simply ablaze with zeal for Christ." This zeal took the form of a passion for work among East End girls. Together with this social activity she combined her boundless enthusiasm for Girl Guide work, and into both she infused a fiery spirit of Catholicism. Though she was to lecture at Hastings, become a Company Captain at Shadwell and study social science and hospital training at the London School of Economics, her most notable work was carried out in the remote regions of Stepney, where she displayed a ruthless compassion in converting factory girls into St. Augustine Girl Guides or their equivalent. In addition to this she set about rescuing other girls from the temptation of "going up west," her intrepid spirit sometimes leading to dramatic pavement tug-of-wars between herself and prospective clients. Parental pride swelled at such unflinching devotion to duty. Sir Henry

Lunn could only stand and admire a missionary heart and stern tenacity of purpose to which he himself had aspired but never realized, while Lady Lunn saw in her daughter's career the vicarious fulfilment of a personal ambition.

A photograph of Eileen Lunn aged about twenty resembles some early pictures of Katherine Mansfield. She had fine simmering eyes with just a glint of humour in them, but her wide and naturally generous mouth is compressed into a thin line and her jaw appears tightly clenched. She never married, but became engaged in 1917 to a vicar in a large manufacturing town, a widower with four children. The following year however she broke off the engagement on the grounds that her health would have prevented the effective discharge of both her marital and social duties, informing her fiancé by letter that they must both accept the sorrow as part of the needed discipline of the soul.

For her health was bad all her life and had been much weakened by the pressure of her strenuous activities. She suffered frequently from minor ailments and in particular from agonizing backache, thought to be due to adhesions following an operation for appendicitis in 1914. So far as was possible she kept all her sorrows and afflictions private, throwing herself back again and again with amazing cheerfulness into her work after each successive operation and convalescence. When, after an operation removing her tonsils, complications set in, and it became evident that her end was near, she consoled her mother and father, assuring them that she was quite happy and not afraid. In a letter to a friend she had declared that introspection was "a very bad thing", adding that one must forget oneself, and this belief helped her to face her death with extraordinary fortitude. At 2.30 on Wednesday morning, August 10th, 1921, worn out by work among the Girl Guides and Brownies of Stepney, her useful life came to an end. She was twenty-four years old.

The Lunns were altogether a talented and remarkable family, and the most remarkable of them, by virtue of his

unique literary achievements, was the second son, Hugh Kingsmill Lunn. Although he knew him to be gifted, Sir Henry
Lunn never really understood the nature of his son's genius,
while Kingsmill was often sorely embarrassed by his father's
social pretensions; and relations between them were in consequence often strained. Even in his early years, which were
spent at 5 Endsleigh Gardens on the northern boundary of
Bloomsbury, he began to react against the Nonconformist-
Evangelical atmosphere of his home life, and undoubtedly his
happiest times were those he spent in Switzerland, where the
family frequently went in connection with the Lunn travel
business and the various other organizations linked with it, such
as the Church Travellers' Club and the Free Church Touring
Guild.

"We were an earnest and upright body of men in these parts
when I was young," Kingsmill told Hesketh Pearson when they
passed through Endsleigh Gardens, some two years before his
death. Apart from his father, whose expanding business and
religious industry was driving the rest of the family into the
narrow upper storeys of the house, there was his godfather,
the Reverend Hugh Price Hughes, round the corner—a fiery
Welsh orator whose ardour in the cause of promoting Social
Purity was whipped by the Parnell case to a pitch of frenzy
which makes W. T. Stead's utterances appear those of a veri-
table libertine. A little further down the road lived Sir Percy
Bunting, editor of the *Contemporary Review*, a monthly
journal dealing exclusively with the problem of social evil, in
a manner which might not have seemed very real to the prostitutes wandering along the far side of the gardens. His sister,
Mrs. Sheldon Amos, was more realistic, and on one notable
occasion at Paddington Station found herself obliged to strike
a Guards officer who had been found guilty of seduction,
crying out at him as she delivered the blow, "You cad!" Besides these public-spirited citizens, there also resided close at
hand a Mr. Algernon Coote, the founder and secretary of the
National Vigilance Association, who saw to it that "girls

coming from the provinces for employment in London should be met on arrival, steered through the multitudinous perils of the street, and penned in a fold where liberty of action was restricted to attending church on Sundays."

Fully conscious of their tremendous responsibilities to the community, when matters of especially grave importance arose, such as the Purification of the Music Halls, one or two of this company would act in collaboration, calling on the Bishop of London to support them. And in emergencies, under the energetic leadership of Sir Henry Lunn, the whole neighbourhood would rise up like a well-trained and formidable army of salvation. On one such occasion, a popular exhibition of paintings by Jules Garnier depicting scenes from Rabelais, they obtained a warrant from Bow Street and descended upon the Galleries at Lower Regent Street in a furniture van, seizing the more outrageous pictures depicting naked monks in bed with naked women, and making off with the intention of consigning them to a glorious but legal conflagration. But even by the turn of the century the climate of opinion was changing, and actions on this scale were regarded as excessive. At a Quarter Session following this episode, Sir Henry Lunn was obliged to read out from the witness-box several carefully chosen extracts from *Gargantua* and *Pantagruel*—passages which Hugh Kingsmill was later to include in his anthology *The High Hill of the Muses* as representing some of his favourite reading. Eventually, the Grand Jury decided that the paintings should be returned to France, where their success was considerable as art which had proved too strong for the English nation.

This, then, was the highly uncongenial background to Kingsmill's early years, against which so much of his life was lived in revolt. "The trouble with reformers," he wrote in *Skye High*, "is that they seldom have any happiness in their natures, and so they can only see what is harmful in a pleasure, never what is beneficial."

To their father's disappointment all three of his sons rejected

orthodox Christianity while still at school, Kingsmill remarking
at the age of twelve that life would be far nicer if his mother
made as many excuses for him as some clergymen did for God.
Sir Henry Lunn seldom lectured his children on Christianity,
but the sufficiency of Christ was in the air continuously. Kingsmill's objection to established religion in general lay in its un-
subtle and uniform unreality. He saw it as simplified humanism;
while humanism, towards which he was naturally far more
attracted, was variegated religion. As an adult he later
developed and clarified the antipathy he felt for organized
Christianity, whatever form it took, in these words: "What I
have felt increasingly for many years is that Christ is simply,
to the Christian, a means of simplifying his emotional experience. The vast area of one's emotions and experiences is
fatiguing and the idea of carrying them into the Absolute
terrifying. Christ is supposed to have provided a guarantee that
he will attend to one's emotional luggage—a kind of valet who
will pack up what's required for a visit to an intimidating noble-
man's seat. . . . The Christ type draws its inspiration from the
conviction that 'no man cometh unto the Father save by Me'."

Throughout his life he felt the weight of the millions who
had narrowed themselves in Christ's name to be increasingly
oppressive, and as he grew up he developed a deeply felt
personal religion which may be summed up in the words of
Polmont, the hero of his story *The End of the World*: "Personal salvation! That was the clue to life. Each man to perfect
himself unobtrusively, without forcing on others a technique
that was perhaps suitable only to himself." He was a mystic,
and could never be said to have conformed completely to any
orthodox form of religion which is out of place in the love of
men and women, whether that love is purely sensual, or, at the
other extreme, the fusion in one of two desires for the happiness
divined beyond this life. Love, he believed, was capable of
expression through earthly passion, but reached beyond this
and could exist without passion, while passion was meaning-
less without love.

The best moments of love, he considered, were not experienced through physical intercourse; but physical attraction was the foundation of an ecstasy which included elements unconnected with the phenomenal world. And since no religious institution incorporates this view in its teaching, the fact that Kingsmill belonged to no such body is understandable. "Systems," he once said, "whatever the philosophy out of which they have grown, necessarily value truth less than victory over rival systems."

Kingsmill's early reaction against puritanism was brought about less by his father, who would take him to Methodist Chapel in the evening, than by his mother, who, as the daughter of a Church of Ireland parson, escorted him to Anglican Church regularly in the morning. She was a far stronger if less colourful character than he, and was directly responsible for creating an austere and forbidding atmosphere about the home which was seldom if ever relaxed in front of her sons.

Sir Henry Lunn grew increasingly engrossed as he became older in ecclesiastical politics. In his social aspirations he was strongly inclined to snobbishness, his snobbery being most apparent in his quite primitive love of titles. As in the case of Barrie, to whom it was a source of constant delight that his private secretary, Lady Cynthia Asquith, should be the daughter of an earl, so Sir Henry Lunn was afforded great pleasure by having in his employment the Hon. Faith Dawnay, and by being surrounded by the fashionable set at Mürren and elsewhere.

But with his obvious shortcomings he was human, sociable, and at times even jovial. His natural sociability, a trait which Kingsmill himself inherited, was in fact particularly pronounced. He would get into conversation with any chance person he met in the course of his many travels, and was incapable of remaining silent, it seems, for more than a minute at a time. He could not even manage to maintain the official two-minute silence, for one November 11th, when Arnold,

Hugh and a friend of Arnold's were standing in the front room of the London office of their firm during the silence, Sir Henry suddenly rushed in, and, seeing the three figures before him grave, unspeaking and immobile, exclaimed, "What's happening? What is it?"

"It *was* the Two Minutes Silence," Arnold replied.

Sir Henry Lunn's dogmatism sprang from absolute religious conviction coupled with a constant desire to live up to his wife's ideals. But she exerted her religious code with all the added severity and virulence of one who feels constantly threatened by vague doubts. She possessed the lifelong habit of suppressing all things difficult or unpleasant to her nature. Thus, questions of finance, of her husband's prosperity or the nature of his business never passed her lips. Sir Henry Lunn was a man for whom one could easily cherish a sympathetic regard, so long as one was not necessarily dependent on him, or involved too closely with him; whereas Lady Lunn was a woman towards whom it would be difficult to entertain any feelings of sympathy or warmth unless one knew her intimately.

Kingsmill seldom spoke of his mother later in his life, and came into contact with her far less than with his father, probably by design rather than accident. It is more than likely that he always felt somewhat apprehensive of her. But despite this later estrangement her influence over him was never fully outgrown during the whole course of his adult life.

2

Schooldays and Holidays

FROM ORLEY FARM, HIS PREPARATORY SCHOOL WHERE HE HAD been reasonably happy, Kingsmill won a scholarship in the summer of 1903, going as a day boy to Harrow. Here he was not so happy, being almost wholly inept at the various sports which formed so intensive a part of public school life, and his discomfort being completed by his status as a mere day boy surrounded by boarders. Later in his life he could recall only one pleasant memory of life at Harrow. This was his first encounter, at the age of sixteen, with the opposite sex. He had met the lady, who was his senior by several years, by accident on a strip of waste land after dark when he was returning home from school. Since he had only fourpence on him at the time and felt that payment on such an occasion should be made on a somewhat more generous scale or not at all, no money changed hands.

Although he disliked examinations and possessed little understanding of such subjects as mathematics, he was more successful at work than at games and on July 1st, 1908, was awarded the Royal Asiatic Society's Public School Gold Medal for his essay *Lord Clive and his Times*.

During these early years Kingsmill suffered from numerous nightmares which, as the world widened round him, grew worse, persisting until he reached fourteen or fifteen. Though he occasionally visited his grandparents in Ireland and Horncastle, most of his long summer holidays were spent in Grindelwald, parts of the nearby countryside of which he thought to be inhabited by the various ogres and demons which appeared in his dreams.

The family at this period was divided into three comparatively separate groups—the "grown-ups", "the boys"—Arnold and Hugh, and the rest—Brian, Eileen and their governess, "Froggy". Arnold and Hugh were great friends as children and would often go off climbing together, a pastime greatly encouraged by their parents as being healthy and wholesome; while Brian, much to his impotent fury, was made to stay behind and play trains with his sister, Eileen. Moving about with strenuous rapidity in the fresh air, it was felt, provided a great safeguard against the unmentionable temptations which advanced with approaching adulthood, and which, for the time being, would not assail Brian. His mother, whose romantic notions and taste for the picturesque affected all her children, used to dress her youngest son in a fancy costume consisting of a brown smock and brown velveteen knickers, and cause him to wear long hair. In the streets he sometimes lifted up his smock to show that he wore knickers like a boy, and was much puzzled by the amusement shown by "Froggy" and her friends over this habit of his.

The two boys', Arnold and Hugh's, love of mountains was of a rather different nature. Arnold's love was based more on knowledge "reasoned, almost respectable;" while Hugh's was founded on a "romantic passion for what is unknown and out of reach." Arnold was intent always on reaching the top of any mountain he set out to climb, and to fail in this objective was a bitter disappointment and defeat to him. His brother, Hugh, cared little if at all whether or not they reached the top, though he would follow Arnold readily even under adverse conditions. How much Kingsmill enjoyed these early expeditions it is impossible to say, for though Arnold was often conscious of a mute but increasing disquiet at the other end of the rope, he never invited his brother's opinion, and Kingsmill for his part never volunteered it.

Their last climb together took place in 1909, when, taking advantage of a trip their father made to Germany, they set out on an ambitious programme for a guideless campaign. While they were scaling Combin de Valsorey in treacherous weather and highly dangerous conditions, their mother down below was receiving large numbers of letters of condolence from friends and relatives sympathizing with her on her tragic loss. The return of the missing sons some while later, after a Press advertisement offering money for the discovery of their corpses, was something of an anti-climax. Kingsmill never climbed again after the breaking up of the partnership with his brother which followed this adventure. "He was," as Arnold put it, "no fanatic."

What appealed to Arnold as a challenge, was for Hugh more of a spectacle. Arnold always experienced a mixture of personal associations and aesthetic emotion when in Switzerland, and was touched to his greatest intensity of feeling when grappling with the intricate difficulties of an ascent, and, those difficulties once overcome, when surveying from the summit the world stretched out below. Arnold's excitement therefore, being more of the will, required physical contact as a necessary means to personal fulfilment; whereas, being more of the imagination, Kingsmill's deepest feelings were stirred not from the top of any mountain but from the bottom and from a distance. For him they held a symbolic beauty unrelated to physical exertion or endeavour, and though personal associations were implicit in his feelings, aesthetic emotions were not. He was always more profoundly moved by the thought of snow-peaks than the sight of them. In *W.J.*, his short story, he puts something of his own mystical view of mountains into the mouth of Gleg, his hero: "Don't you know that the half's greater than the whole, a snow-peak seen beyond a pine-wood clearing lovelier than all the ranges of the world? Why, why, why? . . . because the half suggests infinity; and the whole obscured it, the poor, limited, earthly whole."

The following passage, taken from Kingsmill's unfinished autobiography, gives a beautiful and charming picture of the days he and Arnold spent among the Swiss Alps:

"Arnold and I went up all the lesser mountains . . . rising before dawn and starting off chilly and half-asleep, with a glance up at the tiny hotel on the ridge of the Männlichen to see how clearly it stood out against the thinning darkness. It was our aim to get as high as we could before we came into the sun, which first touched the mountains across the valley and then, passing to the lower summits above our heads, descended the slopes towards us, and suddenly we stepped into it and saw the valley far below, grey and silent. On off days we went to a wood above the village. . . . Outside the wood the insects droned and the air was heavy with the smell of grasses, but it was cool under the pines. There we used to pick bilberries and wild strawberries or lie and listen to the puffing of the little train as it jerked its way up the steep inclines below Alpiglen. The sound died away as the train entered the wood, then some minutes later was heard again, but less laboured, for the worst was over."

On one occasion "the boys" ceremoniously conducted Brian through this wood to a rock about thirty feet high which Arnold had discovered and which was used to practise mountain climbing. After being carefully aided to the summit of this rock by Arnold and Hugh acting as alpine guides, Brian found that he could easily manage the ascent by himself, a discovery which was considered tasteless and out of keeping with his lower station in the family hierarchy.

In his candid and fascinating autobiography, *Switchback,* Brian Lunn has given an interesting synopsis of "the boys", as viewed from his own position as a member of the lower order.

"Arnold's arrogance was more academic, the application at home of the schoolboy paraphernalia of prestige. He took little personal interest in the kids and was a heroic, rather fantastic figure, mountaineer and absent-minded genius. . . . Hugh's bossiness was more human; in matters of common interest he cherished no seniority-prestige. If I was interested by a book he was as ready to discuss it

with me as I was gratified by his attention; we compared
for hours the relative merits of summer and winter holidays, of Grindelwald and Montana, and at an early age
he treated me as an equal sufferer from the pangs of love
when we left a Swiss hotel and the girl of the holidays. . . .
But at the time Arnold's lack of human interest intensified
my admiration for him, while I took Hugh's interest for
granted."

3

Oxford

AT THE AGE OF EIGHTEEN KINGSMILL WON AN EXHIBITION
to New College, Oxford. Here he found that he was expected
to devote two years of his life "to a course of study grouped
round Stubbs's investigations into the local government of our
Anglo-Saxon ancestors." Needless to add he was proof against
the obscure fascination of Stubbs, and with Oxford in general
he was greatly disappointed. As the most famous seat of culture
in the world, he had expected it to hold "the key of a poetic
impassioned enjoyment of life." It did not take him long to
discover his error—"about as long as it would take a man who
went into a hen-house looking for birds of paradise." In
short, he soon came to feel that the intellectual futility of dons
could be divined without two or three years' close study of
them.

At Oxford he succeeded his brother, Arnold, as editor of *The
Isis,* and the essays he wrote in this capacity show clearly how
much contrast rather than comparison stimulated his imagination. Men who react at an early age against their home or
school often find themselves disputing any number of proposi-
tions for the rest of their life, and sometimes indeed placing
themselves in almost untenable positions. Dr. Johnson, Kingsmill's nearest counterpart in history, is a good example of this
tendency; for what poverty was to Johnson, Puritanism was to
Kingsmill.

By this time he had passed through an enthusiasm for
Dickens, whose pathos and panoramic view of the world
appealed to him more than his comedy, and his favourite
authors were Heine and Thackeray. His admiration for both

these is interesting. Heine's weak nature, his practical helplessness and Byronic conceit, all of which Kingsmill was to deplore later in his life, seem to have attracted him on his first encounter as much as the poet's wit and genius. Heine's self-pity and affectation were as bewitching to him at twenty, as his real emotion was breath-taking and he never tired of repeating the lines,

> "Misshandelt und beschimpft zu werden,
> Das ist des Schönen Los auf Erden."

And if Heine's poetry appealed to Kingsmill's youthful romanticism, Thackeray's "rueful disillusioned humour" commended itself to his growing sense of reality. His romanticism to some extent seems to have clogged the early development of this sense of reality, and Thackeray's wavering and uncertain mind impressed him as being more true to life at this period than either Fielding or Shakespeare, a fact which hints at his own irresolute and divided attitude. There is little doubt, too, that this unresolved state of mind acted as a brake to his feelings of eagerness and impatience, and was mainly responsible for his having failed to write any book by the time the war started when he was twenty-five.

The essays he wrote before leaving Oxford are above the average for an undergraduate, but show how in trying to avoid the pitfalls of the many forms of unreality of which he was growing increasingly aware, he often became inconclusive. Here and there, however, appear gleams of that mixture of poetic mysticism and shrewd commonsense which was later to distinguish his writing. Here, for example, is the final paragraph from an essay entitled *The Best Time of One's Life,* which was written in May 1910 :

> "Incidents, whose real importance is illusive rather than real, the first day at school, or at Oxford, the Confirmation ceremony, often a profoundly insignificant event, the day of one's wedding, these are not landmarks in such

a man's life. The thought of them moves him far less than
some fugitive memory, of a quiet sunset, perhaps, beyond
a mountain lake, or of a walk in the early morning taken
long ago in some distant land. Under the influence of such
memories, the make-believe of the many ceased to vex
him. He can even listen with equanimity to those that
prescribe to him the limits that bound the Best Time of
his Life."

Having spent most of his time at Oxford in reading and
conversation, he failed to obtain any degree whatever in his
final examinations and eventually went on to Trinity College
Dublin to rectify the omission.

4

Enter Frank Harris

IN 1910, WHILE KINGSMILL WAS STILL AT OXFORD, FRANK
Harris published *The Man Shakespeare*. It is not difficult to
see why this book fascinated Kingsmill so much. Harris's dis-
similarity to Victorians, dons and Methodists alike was in itself
ample recommendation. He came as a fresh, long-awaited
voice crying from the wilderness and, as Kingsmill wrote, "his
praise of sensuality, special pleading in one who has long since
lost his illusions, sounded melodiously in the ear of youth, and
I hastened to sit at the feet of a master whose message agreed
so well with what I desired from life."

Both Harris and Kingsmill had been affected in the early
part of their lives by Puritanism. In *The Man Shakespeare*
Harris used Shakespeare as a stick with which to beat both the
Puritanism of others on its moral side, and the Puritanism
which lay within himself. Kingsmill, now in the initial toils
of wrestling to escape from the puritanical influence of his
home, was immediately attracted by the flat defiance of the
whole philosophy of Puritanism contained in such a sentence
as, "It may be well for us to learn what infinite virtue lay in
that frail sensual singer." If that was the way to virtue, he
reflected, then he could be counted on to try his hardest. It
was not until much later that he came to realize that Harris's
attitude to literature was, in its inverted Puritanism, closely
related to the attitude to which he himself had been subjected
both as a child at Endsleigh Gardens and as an adolescent
at Harrow where he had been immersed in the late Victorian
reaction against the Puritanism of Dr. Arnold, "with its half-
maudlin, half-barbarous paganism, which made a religion of

games and treated intellect and the love of poetry as effeminate."

In February 1911, after reading Harris's portrait of Carlyle, Kingsmill wrote to him only to have the letter returned from the post-office. Two months later he tried again, expressing the hope that he would do for Heine what he had done for Shakespeare. Harris replied from Nice, thanking him a thousand times for his letter, and enlarging upon the difficulties which dogged every footstep of intelligent and honest writers such as himself. Flattered by the enthusiastic tone of this letter Kingsmill promptly answered, dealing at length with his love of Heine. Despite receiving no reply his ardour remained unabated and in his excessive enthusiasm he seems to have even become temporarily infected with some of Harris's own insensitivity. He had at the time entered for the Shakespeare prize, and a don at London University who was coaching him advised him to have a talk with Sir Israel Gollancz. Sir Israel gave him an appointment and accordingly Kingsmill went down to see him one afternoon at Brondesbury. During their talk, which lasted about an hour, he kept pressing Harris's view that Shakespeare's personal experiences, especially his amorous ones, were reflected throughout his work. In his zeal he quite failed to perceive any signs of uneasiness in the older man. Sir Israel appears to have remained comparatively silent, brooding, and muttering thickly at one point that perhaps there was some personal emotion in *Othello*. Still radiating goodwill towards his host, Kingsmill eventually rose and Sir Israel accompanied him to the door. They shook hands and there was a slight pause. Sir Israel looked as if he had something to say at last. He had. "Young man, what you need is a very good kicking." The door closed abruptly, and a few weeks later Kingsmill failed to get the Shakespeare prize.

By August, after being ploughed for his degree, he retired from hostile criticism to a village in Derbyshire from where he wrote to Harris again, devoting less space to Heine this time. A few days later, on August 28, they met for the first time at the Café Royal for lunch. Harris on this occasion was dressed in a braided overcoat and wore a bowler hat. Broad, but below middle height and standing inside the entrance peering short-sightedly at the persons entering, he struck Kingsmill as so unlike his idea of a bitter impoverished genius and so near to the conventional notion of a Jewish financier that he walked straight past him. But no one else appeared to be waiting there, so retracing his steps, he approached and asked, "Mr. Frank Harris?" Harris's diffident air vanished, he grasped the new disciple's hand and uttered his first words to him: "There is an excellent wine at the Savoy I want you to taste!"

After lunch, which was largely taken up with Harris's accounts of himself as a labourer, librarian, railwayman, writer, etc., they went along to Dan Rider's bookshop off St. Martin's Lane. This, in the three or four years before the first World War, was the meeting place for a number of writers, painters and journalists: Joseph Simpson, Claude Lovat Fraser, Kenneth Hare, Middleton Murry, Katherine Mansfield, Harold Weston, Haldane Macfall, Holbrook Jackson and others, most of whom at one time or another were admirers of Harris. Later, after tea with Mrs. Harris at Stewart's, they drove to Roehampton where Harris was then living. The end of this highly successful day was perhaps a little jarring. After dinner Kingsmill walked down Putney Hill with Harris and his wife. "In my exhilaration I was swinging my stick," he records, "and it struck Mrs. Harris's lap-dog, who was taking the air with us. The poor brute suffered for forty-eight hours as a result of the blow, which was typical of the clumsiness I always displayed in everything which concerned Mrs. Harris."

His veneration for the master did not long survive this first meeting, but became increasingly confused in the months that followed, and by August 1912 he was no longer an adoring disciple, but had become instead Harris's humdrum assistant on *Hearth and Home*, "a blameless ladies' journal which did not long survive the ordeal of being edited by Harris."

The patronage which Harris extended to his band of admirers seems to have been largely influenced by the size of their fathers' bank balance. It was Claude Lovat Fraser's father, a wealthy solicitor, who purchased *Hearth and Home,* Harris agreeing beforehand to contribute five hundred pounds of the purchase money himself and his failure to produce this sum being one of the main causes of the bitter dissentions which culminated, the following spring, with the collapse of the paper. Sir Henry Lunn, in Harris's view, might have been good for unlimited free travel. Indeed it was Sir Henry who secured for him a free passage to America on a German boat for his lecture tour in November 1912. "Your father really is a brick," Harris told Kingsmill once the passage was arranged. A more awe-inspiring note was struck a month later towards the close of Harris's highly unsuccessful tour. "Arrange for me to get my passage back free," he wired Kingsmill, "it might help us." Unfortunately Sir Henry Lunn and Harris did not respond with any marked degree of warmth to each other's company, and when they met to discuss plans for a cruise to India for the Durbar, Harris claiming at the time to know the Gaekwar of Baroda who was anxious to act as his host out in India, their impressions of one another were unenthusiastic. "I didn't like the way he tried to flatter me," Sir Henry Lunn said afterwards; and Harris told Kingsmill, "I could have helped your father, but. . . ."

The mild antipathy Harris felt for Sir Henry Lunn was soon extended to his son in a more violent form. From various tasteless remarks it must have become clear even to Harris that Kingsmill's once infinite admiration for him had lately undergone severe qualification. While Harris was lecturing in America, Kingsmill had been voted on to the board of *Hearth and Home* to safeguard Harris's interests during his absence. Ignorant until then of the profound and intricate policies which circulated round a ladies' weekly journal endeavouring to remain breathing under the weight of Harris's management, he was as Harris's personal representative in an embarrassing position, and was much disconcerted to find even his appointment the theme of violent opinions.

When Harris returned, Kingsmill was informed through Dan Rider that he was no longer to be paid for reviewing books, and then, some weeks later, that he was not to sell books he had reviewed. His only job, besides continuing these reviews gratis, was to record his vote in favour of Harris at all Board Meetings. His reaction to this state of affairs was promptly to send in his resignation, to which Harris, equally promptly, replied with four pages of abuse. This was in February 1913, and Harris and Kingsmill did not meet again for fourteen years.

It may have been that Harris's sudden cooling towards Kingsmill was due in part to Mrs. Harris's influence. But Harris later accused him of stirring the office boy on *Hearth and Home*, Sweetapple by name, to open mutiny. Sweetapple, "as imperturbable as Lord Balfour though only fourteen," as Kingsmill described him, was one of the few members of the office staff who did not fear Harris. On one occasion he was combing his hair, a pocket mirror in his hand, when the door burst open and Harris entered. Sweetapple threw him a glance and went on combing, and Harris, glaring fiercely back at him as he passed, strode quickly through, without a smile, into his office—though not before he heard Kingsmill burst into a volley of loud laughter. Anyone who knows the volume of Kingsmill's laughter will immediately extend their sympathy to Harris over this incident. Fourteen years later Harris had not forgotten it and wrote an account of the event in a letter to Hesketh Pearson. "I said to Lunn," he concluded, "that by such methods he would end in the gutter."

Hearth and Home makes curious reading during the time of Harris's editorship. Some effort was obviously made to hold the same public as had welcomed the journal each week into their homes during past years. A number of the regular features still appeared, such as *Gowns and Gossip, In Quest of Beauty* and *Stitches in Time*. The *Movements of Royalty* were still fully reported. There was still the "Home Advice" page, where Mrs. Talbot Cooke and Mrs. Langton Bayly would urge "Mourne" to trust her loose covers to Messrs. John Barker & Co., High St., Kensington. In the "Health and Beauty" page, Dame Deborah Primrose continued to warn "Moorland Nymph" that, contrary to what some vulgar advertisements seemed to suggest, it was not in accord with true beauty to have too pronounced a bust, and to explain to "Daffodil" how to reduce the prominence of her hips, should this prominence be due to fatness and not merely large bones. Still flourishing too, was the *Hearth and Home* Guild of Aid for Distressed Gentle-people which could boast of eighteen patronesses, fifteen of them titled, a committee of eleven other ladies scarcely less exalted, not to mention a chairman, treasurer and honorary solicitors and occulists galore, whose aim was to provide "monthly allowances, special grants when necessary, also clothing and other benefits for persons of *gentle birth* who have fallen on necessitous circumstances." The gifts made to this Guild consisted of regular donations of money, suitably adver-tised, from the patronesses and committee members, and other more varied contributions from the general public, among which were old boots, stamps, parcels of waistcoats, infants' nightgowns, and a bust of Dante.

But the additions made to these regular items were some-times inharmonious. *Sense and Nonsense in the Press* was devoted almost entirely to attacking well-known public figures. *French Women's Best Virtues* (kindness and tidiness) and *Should Women wear Corsets?* by a Lover of Fair Play both somehow struck a wrong note and may be attributable to a German ex-hairdresser whom Harris gave a free hand in the paper before getting rid of him at the general request after some two or three weeks of chaos. Another discord was sounded perhaps by the large advertisement for Sir Henry Lunn's travel agency, which squeezed the other lesser advertisements for corsets, cots and designs for fancy dress to the very peri-meter of the page, forming there a curious frame to the still undaunted if somewhat puzzled features of Sir Henry Lunn himself which stare out from the centre.

Into this strange medley Harris himself occasionally erupted with an article on food, or an open letter to the Home Secretary on imprisonment for debt, or "A Romance from the Life of Dostoevsky" or again a criticism of Meredith or Woodrow Wilson. Some of his pieces bore headings which one would more readily associate with the *News of the World* today. For instance :

FEEBLE-MINDED CHILDREN FLOGGED AT LEICESTER
Why shouldn't we flog our pimples?

Although he wrote one short story, *The Reluctant Ghost,* Kingsmill's main contributions consisted of book reviews and interviews. Among titles of books sent to him were *The Girl Scout, Her Convict Husband, Catching a Coronet, Every Man's Desire* and *The Day Book for Busy Men and Women.* Of one book written to further the woman's movement he wrote in conclusion : "This is a very fine book, and perhaps the author will give us an even finer one when she realizes that men as well as women are aiming at the production of a higher type."

The most important of his interviews were those with W. B. Yeats, G. K. Chesterton and Hugh Walpole. They were all competently done, but perhaps because of the public for whom he was writing, none of them is exceptional. More amusing are some of the less important ones such as *The Work of a Telephone Operator.* His object was, as he put it, "if possible to interview a telephone operator." But this task proved less simple than may be supposed, for arriving at the headquarters of the London Telephone Service, he was regarded with extreme suspicion by the authorities and his request was peremptorily refused. Instead he spoke to a certain Miss Heap, the Superintendent, who read out to him a list of the regulations. This completed, she escorted him round the building. "The efficiency of the organization was obvious," he wrote, "but there was something depressing in the sight of all those young girls fettered to such a routine task." After refuting the theory that the telephone operator is an "indolent, lordly creature who attends to distracted business men whenever she can tear herself away from her novel and her chocolates," he concluded by regretting that the work held no joy for its own sake and no chance of individual expression, "as in the middle ages."

At the end of this article there appears a curt note by Frank Harris : "Any criticism of fact or opinion in this article will be welcomed."

Sometimes such criticism was forthcoming in most alarming forms. After Kingsmill had pleaded in an interview with Mrs. Maud Churton, for greater sincerity and a bolder attitude towards love, one of the women readers turned up at the office armed with an umbrella for his personal chastisement. The interview with Mrs. Maud Churton, who described herself simply as "a good mother", but who was the author of *Modern Marriage, Downward*, and *The Love Seeker*, took place near Hendon and is highly entertaining to read. Not least of the entertainment is provided by extracts from the novelist's own books. "The candid and generous nature of her books", Kingsmill wrote, "must encourage other women to be true to themselves," and, he might have added, untrue to their husbands.

"Why do women admire soldiers and sailors so much?" he asked during the course of the interview.

"Do they? . . . I remember, when I stayed in a foreign station, how shocked I was at the freedom with which English officers mentioned women's names—and the way they spoke of them! Once as I was crossing a field with an officer during manoeuvres, he said to me, pointing out some ladies of the garrison, 'Who are those females?' No artist could have spoken like that."

One other of Kingsmill's articles for *Hearth and Home* deserves mention. The article in question, on Cheltenham College was based on the impressions of a girl friend who, some four years previously, had left Cheltenham rather abruptly. "No allowance seems to have been made for the difference between girls and boys," he complained incredulously. "Cheltenham aims at producing manly girls as Eton aims at producing manly boys." Down at Cheltenham itself, this edition of *Hearth and Home* was sold out in a couple of hours, and Miss Faithfull, the principal, convened her colleagues to discuss what steps should be taken. The outcome of their deliberations was an article which appeared a few weeks later : "Cheltenham Ladies' College : An Appreciation by an Old Pupil." In this article which set out to prove that Cheltenham produced womanly women, Miss A. Isabel Philips, the old pupil in question, concluded : "I do not want to create an impression of 'goody-goodness' about Cheltenham, or to give an idea of hard work and no play. . . . I suppose that the playing fields belonging to Cheltenham Ladies' College would compare favourably with those of any boys' school and were certainly quite as much used."

5

Prisoner of War

WITH THE BEGINNING OF THE WAR KINGSMILL ENLISTED AS A
private in a regiment of cyclists, and in the autumn of 1914
received a commission in the Royal Naval Volunteer Reserve.
The following year saw his marriage to Miss Eileen Fitzgerald
Turpin with whom he settled down near Blandford, where
he was stationed.

Although he had picked up a lot of information about sex
from Frank Harris and, as Hesketh Pearson puts it, "one piece
of knowledge with which he could have dispensed," Kingsmill
remained curiously naïve in some aspects all his life. In the
early summer of 1915, both he and his wife were, to use his
own words, "apprehensive about children," so when early one
morning Eileen thought their fear was at last realized, she
begged him to run to seek the advice of the nearest doctor
whom, together with his spinster sister, they had just met
socially. Feeling as yet unconvinced, he tried to reason her
fears away, but such sense as he possessed was soon overborne,
his wife stressing how kind the doctor had seemed and how
eager he would doubtless be to render all his professional
assistance. Dressing hurriedly Kingsmill then set out, bewildered
but resolute, his feet ringing sharply through the streets of the
silent, sleeping town. On reaching the doctor's house, a com-
modious residence standing in its own grounds, he paused
uncertainly. No light shone from any of the windows, and all
was still. Setting his jaw he pulled forcefully at the bell which
reverberated loudly through the house, but no one stirred
until he had rung with added vigour twice more. Then a win-

dow suddenly went up and a voice barked out sharply, "Who's that?" Kingsmill backed a few paces from under the portico over the front door, took up his position on a grass plot opposite, and glancing uneasily at the other dark windows for any sign of the spinster sister, he began and sustained the following dialogue at the top of his voice.

"I had the pleasure of meeting you the other day."

"Speak up. I can't hear."

"My name is——"

"I know, I know."

"I'm most frightfully sorry to disturb you, but my wife is afraid she has—conceived."

"What?"

"Conceived. My wife's worried, upset. She thinks something may have happened."

"I don't know what you're talking about."

"It's my wife. She's very upset. We don't know what to do. I wondered if you would care to——"

"I'll see you in the morning."

The window went down with a bang, and Kingsmill described his journey home as uneventful.

Apart from these difficulties, his wife was desperately anxious that he should not be sent abroad, threatening to kill herself, if he were, and so, "for reasons more complex than the simple aversion from physical violence, naturally assumed by others to be the sole possible explanation for remaining at home," he did not leave England until November 1916. Then his battalion left for Boulogne, thence to Calais where they remained some few days before starting off once more, this time to the neighbourhood of Rue, near the mouth of the Somme.

While here, the company commander suddenly went on leave, relinquishing his post temporarily to Kingsmill. "It is difficult to praise oneself," he comments in his readable and amusing war memoirs, *Behind Both Lines,* and so, he proceeds, he asked Pound, a fellow-officer, for any memories of his accomplishments in this elevated position. Pound's reply casts some doubts, perhaps, on Kingsmill's military capabilities.

"You used," he said, "to give your orders for the day from your bed. They were taken by the sergeant-major, leaning through the window. On one occasion when you were supposed to inspect the guard, you didn't like the idea of going through the mud, so you sent for the guard, and inspected them through the doorway, in slippers, with a newspaper under your arm. I don't remember anything else, except that when a Tommy was once singing 'The roses round the door, Make me love my mother more,' you asked him to explain why the roses round the door should make him care more for his mother, and the poor chap didn't know what to say."

Throughout his military career, which seems to have been of a curiously informal nature, Kingsmill never showed signs of developing into a vigorous disciplinarian. Soon the battalion moved up to Le Crotoy, where more serious training took place, various mock attacks being practised "with as close an approximation to the real thing as was consistent with the absence of an enemy and the presence of a general."

By the middle of January they had reached the front. Southwood, an officer in Kingsmill's battalion, has left a portrait of him in a letter to his wife written at this time.

"He has more individuality perhaps, than any man in the battalion," Southwood wrote, "he has a very sympathetic nature, but at times, through thoughtlessness, gives the impression of being selfish . . . he is one of those people whom nature never intended to live in a confined space. . . . If he does not knock over the candle, he upsets the table and scatters the food all over the floor. Failing either of these little acts he kicks the brazier over, or looks for a stud he has not lost, carefully holding a dripping candle over your tunic all the time. He has other little ways such as dropping jam on the petrol can which we use for sitting on, or snatching away the only light just as one is negotiating a difficult corner, in the desire to find his fountain-pen which he is holding all the time in his left hand. . . ."

Presently the battalion advanced in support of two other battalions in a brigade attack which was planned to last some eight minutes, but which in fact was prolonged for some fifty hours of continuous fighting. Fairly early on, during the night, Kingsmill, who appears to have been wandering around far ahead of his company, noticed, not for the first time, a group of German soldiers near at hand. "At the same moment they saw me. I ran another four or five paces, and tripped up. When I got to my feet, they had surrounded me, and I handed them my revolver."

He was led back behind the German lines quoting Heine to his captors, possibly in an endeavour to make his peaceful intentions quite clear to them. Overcoming the natural sting he was suffering "under the double stigma of being out of the war, and being out undamaged," he records that "it was a glorious night, and as I looked up at it, I suddenly realized that the war was over for me, the curtain of death rolled up, and life stretched out before me once more."

But his time at Karlsruhe prison camp, where he was sent for a period of fourteen months, had none of the delights of normal life. Worst of all his privations, he felt, was the lack of any women. "How sick one got of one's own sex!" he complained, "Men, men, men, always men!" Another hardship was the food, especially before the Red Cross parcels began to arrive.

> But what is life? One day an empty belly
> The next an overdose of shrimps in jelly.

It was at Karlsruhe that he met John Holms, a melancholy, literate though mainly inarticulate, self-confessed genius who remained his friend, much to many of his other friends' surprise, until his, Holms's, death in January 1934. Many people who met Holms were of the opinion that he was a complete charlatan; and with good reason, for he seldom uttered an original remark, seldom for that matter completed a sentence. But undoubtedly there was something genuine buried within him which occasionally in his early years while a prisoner of war found release, but which became increasingly obscured as he grew older. The late Edwin Muir who met Holms shortly after the war was much impressed by him, and while granting that he did not possess "the rich spontaneous genius of Hugh Kingsmill" nevertheless regarded him as the most remarkable man he had ever met. But to reduce this last unqualified judgment to more realistic proportions, one should perhaps add that a strain of naïvety seems to have intermingled with the charm and intelligence of Edwin Muir's nature. Malcolm Muggeridge has suggested that Kingsmill's own regard for Holms was "due to the fact that he represented the exact converse of Methodism and Sir Henry Lunn." This is certainly true, but temperamentally they were not so unsuited as may be supposed, and a friendship which might never have prospered amid the hubbub of ordinary life sprang up during the weary hours at Karlsruhe, where they would discuss literature through many an afternoon and evening over a few glasses of wine, when through the increasing mellowness "past happiness revived and future happiness ceased to be problematical."

Part of Holms's appeal for Kingsmill may have been due to the fact that he was constantly at loggerheads with his father, a very capable administrator in the Indian Civil Service from whom, in Kingsmill's view, he inherited what was tough and unexpressive in his nature. His more attractive qualities, his gentleness and also his melancholy, came from his mother, who was descended from John Ferrar, brother of Nicholas Ferrar, the founder of a religious community at Little Gidding in the seventeenth century. This community spent their waking hours in repeating or singing without interruption the maximum number of psalms and hymns. Isaac Walton, in his *Life of George Herbert*, has described these activities. "And it is to be noted," he writes, "that in this continued serving of God, the Psalter or the whole book of Psalms, was in every four and twenty hours sung or read over, from the first to the last verse: and this was done as constantly as the sun runs his circle every day about the world, and then begins the instant that it ended. Thus did Mr. Ferrar and his happy family serve God day and night."

"It is not fanciful," Kingsmill commented, "to assign some of the weight which lay on Holms's spirits to this ancestral treadmill."

At the same time he detected an "intense capacity for happiness" under Holms's melancholy and self-absorption, while it is evident from Kingsmill's novels that a strong undercurrent of melancholia ran through his own more overwhelming and affectionate nature. This melancholia was similar in some respects to Johnson's, but owing to his far better health, Kingsmill overcame it much more successfully than Johnson in the course of his daily life. Possibly aware of this, he used later in life to retire to bed and fast periodically—an obscure method of keeping up one's spirits for anyone not nurtured on Puritanism.

Holms's mellow dreaminess appealed naturally to Kingsmill, and stirred him to feelings of poetry, a fact which comes out in many passages in *Behind Both Lines,* for example.

"May was a fine month, and Holms and I spent most of the day reading under the chestnut trees. In the long calm evenings the idea of escape attracted us. Switzerland was not far away, and we pictured ourselves wandering through fields, by the smooth-flowing Rhine, under a full moon, each day nearer the mountains, which would come faintly into view as we approached the frontier."

It is in human nature to parade one's faults under the guise of personal accomplishments. Holms filled the void between his potential self-development and his lack of practical achievement with an air of insincerity and bluff, suggesting an impenetrable sagacity not capable of being confined within the laws of language. It was this defence, unaggressive yet unassailable which, superimposed on his semi-paralysed temperament, stifled his powers of self-expression. Mere vanity on its own, however abnormal, can never be the sole reason for such silence any more than it can be the only incentive to produce great literature. Somewhere, in the depths of Holms's complex nature, crushed yet never wholly extinct, something genuine and noble struggled vainly to free itself. Memory of early years might sometimes recall fleeting moments of eager enthusiasm when his eyes would shine again with young and unspoilt emotion; but these moments were few and fragmentary and all too soon the tragedy of his life weighed down upon his spirit once more, and all their elusive magic was lost.

It is not difficult to understand why, under such circumstances, people's opinions differed so widely as to Holms's true character. For it was as easy to romanticize upon his hidden and unknown qualities as it was to satirize his superficiality and inertia. Failures of one kind or another will always attract the widest controversy.

Holms placed a great and lasting value on Kingsmill's friendship, and as the shades of despair closed in around him, he came to feel that from no one else could he receive a genuine appreciation and deep affection.

"I am sure," he wrote to Kingsmill in a letter shortly after the war, "that neither of us will ever meet anyone else in life who could supply one quarter of what has made our friendship. As I told you, in my last letter, the whole of these six months when suicide has hardly been out of my brain for 24 hours I have thought of you as my only refuge in life . . . I should certainly have killed myself before now if you had not been in the world."

Holms possessed little vitality, was self-pitying and self-preoccupied, and lacked the necessary confidence to overcome these difficulties. From what little he wrote one can see, in addition, that he was sensitive, intelligent, and had a fine appreciation of literature, although in his literary criticism he was inclined to indulge his sense of power. From Kingsmill he hoped to obtain a profound pity for his predicament. Kingsmill was usually more at ease with people who were counted as failures in the world, and having had his own self-confidence weakened earlier in life, was genuinely sympathetic towards Holms. In return for this sympathy he demanded from Holms an unstinted appreciation of his own novels which he could find nowhere else. Holms realized Kingsmill's need as clearly as Kingsmill realized his, and the criticisms he gave of *The Will to Love*, *The Dawn's Delay* and *Blondel* were composed of a mixture of sound and imaginative perception, interspersed with hyperboles of praise. The assertion, for example, at one point that there was no writer of modern fiction equal to Kingsmill from a man who at the same time confessed that he read few current novels, is worthless as criticism. But, in his need for encouragement, Kingsmill never objected to such extravagance, but drank it in thirstily and reserved his excited irritation for any minor qualification by which Holmes occasionally would see fit to fetter his enthusiasm.

Kingsmill seems to have attracted persons who were of weak disposition or who, temporarily at least, were suffering from acute despondency. Such people appeared able to sense instinctively that while he would feel sorry for them, he possessed that type of sympathy which minimized their sorrow or disappointment and did not swell it by gloomy indulgence. This kind of dependence can be extremely gratifying in its initial stages, but soon grows increasingly wearisome. Yet although Kingsmill came to regard Holms as "a bit of a bluffer" he seldom made any impatience he may have felt apparent to his friend. He was always benevolent and concerned with Holms's lack of vitality and unresolved character until the end of his life. His partiality and stamina in dealing with such problems suggest that he may have found alleviation from his own troubles and perplexities in the contemplation of other people's.

This view is supported by the pattern of later events. Although they did not often meet after the war, Kingsmill and Holms corresponded frequently and at length until the late 1920's, at which time Kingsmill had lost his money and was

living in comparative penury. Their friendship was then subjected to a severe financial strain, for about this time too, Holms
while staying at St. Tropez, had met Peggy Guggenheim, that
notoriously wealthy American woman, itinerant searcher after
modern art treasures and new husbands. In her two volumes
of reminiscences, *Out of this Century* and *Confessions of an
Art Addict*, Peggy Guggenheim has displayed a gift, similar
perhaps in its own way to that of André Gide or even Benvenuto Cellini, for presenting the public with melodramatic
confessions without at the same time revealing the truth. *Out
of this Century* the first, the most entertaining and uninhibited
of her efforts, was hurriedly bought up by the various members
of her family who did such a thorough job that it is now
virtually unobtainable. One short extract dealing with her
life with Holms may explain the energy they put into this
task :

". . . and I had sinned not once, but many times. I often
wondered how they knew. The only place this fact was ever
recorded was in my diary, where I had written, 'fighting all
day, f—— all night'. . . ."

In her second attempt at autobiography she was more reticent. She did not, for example, see fit to reveal the date of
her birth, which took place probably in the summer of 1898.
But she gave a lively enough account of her many eccentric
and even mentally unbalanced ancestors. Turning abruptly to
her own life she recorded that, while still a child, she fell
heavily on her head while out riding in a park; and a little
later we find her paying the inevitable visit to a psychologist
to discover whether or not she was losing her mind. His answer
was pertinent and direct : he asked her, "Are you sure you have
a mind to lose?" As an adult, that is, after she came into her
fortune, her life appears up to the present to have been a succession of fiancés and husbands, legal and unofficial, ranging
from flying-officers to novelists, and of impoverished artists to
whom she had very generously acted as patron. Together these
are instanced as evidence of her own superabundant and in-

satiable appetite for life, rather than the common need of numerous impecunious men for funds.

Peggy Guggenheim first met John Holms during 1928 in a bistro at St. Tropez. Although not feeling very happy that evening, she succeeded in executing a wild and abandoned dance upon one of the tables. The underlying conflict of emotions and activity in this performance seems to have impressed the thoughtful Holms, who then led her away to a nearby tower where he lightly kissed her. "This certainly impressed me," she recorded, "and I can attribute everything that followed to this simple little kiss. . . ."

Briefly what followed was that Holms married the woman with whom he had for some time been living and then dispatched his new wife back to the West of England, himself joining Peggy Guggenheim as an unofficial husband. For the next year or two they wandered together across Europe, going first to Avignon where Peggy Guggenheim made what she describes as a "symbolic gesture", lightly tossing her wedding ring from her balcony into the street, but regretting her action even before the ring had struck the pavement as "it was such a nice little ring, and I have found myself so often in need of one."

She seems to have been fascinated by the air of mystery on the surface of Holms's personality, and her attraction for him was consequently centred around her lack of knowledge of him. "I don't know what he expected from me," she confessed with all the pathos of the affluent, "but I don't think he was disappointed." Nor did Kingsmill think so, though he was less doubtful over what it was that Holms wanted. "I saw Holms in Paris three weeks ago," he wrote to Lance Sieveking from Munich in July 1930, "he was in a very comfortable roomy flat. A rich American woman sees to it that when he asks for bread he shall get it fresh."

Kingsmill, who liked Peggy Guggenheim approximately as little as she liked him, did not approve of the effect that this desirable state of affairs was having on his friend.

"In return," he continued, "he has become a competent chauffeur and motors her round Europe. It was 8 a.m. when I roused him. He peered out a little fretfully in white silk pyjamas edged with pink; finally he dressed and accompanied me to the P.L.M. I asked him why he didn't write. He sighed. 'Life is—er—rather difficult.' I'm afraid he'll never do anything. He has lost his old intensity and gloom and seems merely preoccupied with being comfortable. But he is so unaccountable that he may take another turn later."

But he gave no real sign of taking another turn, although towards the end of his life he was again closer to Kingsmill. Possibly Peggy Guggenheim had begun to get a little fed up with his mysterious air after a while, for by the beginning of 1933 she was "physically and secretly in love" with one of his friends whom she later left on his becoming a communist.

In January 1934 Holms died suddenly while under an anaesthetic for a minor operation to a broken wrist. "Poor old Holms," Kingsmill remarked to Lance Sieveking when breaking the news to him. "It was merely a little operation in the wrist, perfectly simple, but he didn't come round from the anaesthetic. Poor old Holms. Bloody shame."

*   *   *

At Karlsruhe, Kingsmill took a normal active part in the prison life, speaking at debates and writing a few theatricals which were performed by the prisoners "to the agonized applause of five hundred compulsory celibates." In addition to this he wrote his first novel, *The Will to Love*. Lance Sieveking, the novelist, who was a fellow prisoner at Karlsruhe, has given a picture of Kingsmill at work on this book.

He used to write, "in the Appel hut at Karlsruhe. There he sat, crouched over the rickety table working with happy concentration, slowly covering the sheet with his small neat handwriting while all about him a cheerful hubbub filled the air; four men just behind him playing ping-pong; two men wrestling; a man with a very loud unmusical voice singing. . . .

"More than once I saw Hughie look up with a pained expression during a lull in the din.

" 'Don't stop, old man!' he would shout to the pair at the piano, and then reproachfully to the resting ping-pong players : 'I say! You're not giving up, are you?' And then to me, or anyone standing near, in a semi-confidential tone : 'I find it helps me to concentrate, y'know, old man'."

In April 1918 Kingsmill left Karlsruhe for Mainz, where he remained until returning to England in November the same year. The chaplain at Karlsruhe noted Kingsmill's rather self-conscious departure thus :

"It was a really quaint sight to see Lunn, rooted out after a year here, gazing in dismay at his masses of stuff, and at a loss how to proceed, and then emerging with a crumpled hat, far too small, crammed on his head, looking less like a soldier than anyone I have ever seen, and quite unable to understand why everyone smiled. But the clouds soon passed away, and his hearty laugh was the last thing heard as he rolled out."

In the favourable conditions such as Kingsmill experienced, where the camp authorities left the prisoners to themselves, captivity is among the lesser evils of war. "But the perpetual confinement," he wrote some years later, "the perpetual society of one's own sex, and the consciousness of being a dead weight are more wearing than one realizes at the time, and usually require a year or so to recover from them. Taken in one stretch, the twenty-one months of my captivity were too many by quite half, but I have often thought since how satisfactory it would have been had I been able to bank them and draw two or three weeks whenever I wanted a respite from ordinary existence."

6

"The Will to Love"

On his eventual return to England Kingsmill was stationed for a few weeks at Badajos Barracks at Aldershot, where he delivered a series of lectures. The nature of these lectures, as might be expected, were literary rather than military. Having unearthed about thirty copies of Ballantyne's *The Coral Island,* he circulated them round his pupils who read it out in turn while he attempted to draw plans of the island on a black-board. The tale itself pleased him less than it pleased his audience. "Dire rot the book is," he remarked, "with reflections about the goodness of the Creator in providing bread-fruit trees for the shipwrecked. The men, however, do not seem vexed."

Shortly after his release from the army he went to stay for a time with his uncle Holdsworth Lunn, who was running a number of Scottish hotels. The next month or two was spent at the Allan Water Hotel at the Bridge of Allan. During the morning he would attend his uncle rather in the manner of an A.D.C. but his afternoons were left free for him to read, write letters to various literary periodicals and a poem in caricature of A. R. Orage to *The New Age,* and to work on the stories which were to form *The Dawn's Delay.* These days were diversified, too, by a good many amusing incidents, illustrating the underworld of hotel management—"some priceless letters to the manageress from a sacked housemaid, an outburst of Bolshevism among two locker boys, etc."

But there existed at this time a general feeling both in the nothern and southern branches of the business that he would be happier elsewhere, and his father, who was conferring at the time with the Mayor of Stratford, Archibald Flower, about the possibility of a War Memorial in Stratford which would give the town an increased business, suddenly had the inspiration that his second son would be happiest of all at Shakespeare's birthplace. His fertile mind rapidly transformed the Stratford War Memorial scheme into a rest hostel for American visitors to be run by Kingsmill. That year Stratford was being threatened by a strong Bolshevik element which wanted to start up factories and get rid of Shakespeare, whose actual birthplace some of the extremists had tried to storm, and to safeguard the town Sir Henry Lunn formed the Stratford-on-Avon Preservation Committee. The Town Council, was hostile to the enterprise and at a truly extraordinary general meeting put some searching questions to Sir Henry. In a circular entreating the public to subscribe one hundred thousand pounds towards a Stratford War Memorial, he had referred to Stratford as "the Mecca of every Englishman." But pressed by the Chairman of the Town Council to give the date of his first visit to this Mecca, he had to name a day in the previous month.

Response to Sir Henry's appeal was meagre for, as Kingsmill explained, "people were getting rather tired of putting money into the pockets of the living in order to testify their gratitude to the dead." About this time, with the public listless, the Committee unhelpful and the Council openly hostile, Kingsmill arrived from Scotland to a welcome he described as "a little languid." However, he was invited to dinner by Flower one evening before a performance of *Julius Caesar*. Sir Johnstone Forbes-Robertson, William Archer and Harold Child were stopping with Flower, and Kingsmill returned with them after the play. Before the performance the conversation had flagged, but now they were relaxed and amiable, greeting Forbes-Robertson's, "What a fellow Shakespeare was! He knew his mob—ha! ha! ha!" with a gracious acquiescence which allowed Shakespeare, in spite of everything, to be as experienced and knowledgeable as themselves.

Stratford was crowded out for the Festival, and Kingsmill

was lodged in a large building with between two and three hundred female elementary school-teachers, whom the Morris Dance and Folk Lore resurrectionist, Cecil Sharp, had, by some extraordinary means, "trepanned into sacrificing their holidays to the business of recapturing movements and sounds which had welled spontaneously out of the yokels of the Middle Ages."

Kingsmill's stay at Stratford seems to have been fairly pleasant, relaxing and informal. Sometimes in the morning he would visit the Shakespeare Memorial Library where he had got to know the librarian. At other times he would saunter along to have a talk with the founder of the Shakespeare Head Press, A. H. Bullen, himself a poet, and the two of them would repair to a pleasant old inn over the way from the Press. And some afternoons he would visit some local dignitary and anxiously discuss over tea the anti-Shakespearean feeling on the Town Council.

The financial response engendered by these methods fell somewhat short of the target. All in all five hundred pounds out of the hundred thousand was amassed, the enterprise was then abandoned and Kingsmill left Stratford.

During these months *The Will to Love* was published, this being the only one of his books to be written under the name of Hugh Lunn. He had first sent it to Katherine Mansfield, who praised it generously, but added a somewhat strange rider to the effect that his humour tended in places to get out of rein. An example of the type of remark to which she objected is given by a minor character in the book, an undergraduate, who asks at one point, "If women refrain from writing poems because they are poems, and from painting pictures because they are pictures, are we to assume that they abstain from mechanical invention because some of them resemble steam-rollers?"

The story tells of a young and intelligent girl, Barbara, in some respects similar to H. G. Wells's "advanced" heroine, Anne Veronica, who is seduced by a much older man, Ralph

Parker, the leading male figure in the novel who is based on the character of Frank Harris. There is little sense of real love between them, for Barbara in pursuing Parker is chasing an idea, trying to corner life. But her seduction, Vincent Brome assures us in his recent biography of Harris, closely follows the pattern of many of Harris's conquests. Ralph Parker's love-making involves an abundance of talk, both about himself and about the girl in question—"then as the wind drops before the rain pours down, silence, and the first kiss .The rest according to routine."

The character of Barbara is roughly based on that of Enid Bagnold, who had worked with Kingsmill on *Hearth and Home*. Hugh Kingsmill himself appears early on in the book in the minor character of Roderick Cory, a clever, witty man whose essential sensitiveness is concealed often under a mask of irony. But no one takes much notice of his opinions, be they ever so penetrating—an accurate if somewhat complacent prognostication of Kingsmill's own fate. A technical flaw in the novel is the early disappearance of Roderick Cory, who does not again enter the book, though Kingsmill himself makes a brief re-appearance as Cyril Mears, a young undergraduate.

Owing to the fact that it was written in a prisoner of war camp, partially secluded from the many distractions and harrowing emotional disturbances of normal day to day life, this book has a detachment which none of his later long novels were ever to achieve. It was to further this spirit of detachment that Kingsmill made the central character a young girl. But in doing this he created a difficulty, which he never successfully overcame. The main figure in all his novels and some of his short stories resembles to a large degree himself, and as *The Will to Love* proceeds Barbara steadily grows less like Anne Veronica or Enid Bagnold and more like Hugh Kingsmill. Her witty retorts are his; her immediate poetic response to nature is his; the literary expression of her thoughts is his; the emotions felt while travelling in a train by night are again his; even her feelings after her love-affair with Ralph Parker is

over have something in common with Kingsmill's own disillusionment with Frank Harris as a literary master. Kingsmill obviously felt this central difficulty in the book, which he
tried, unsuccessfully, to brush aside in a couple of sentences :

"Barbara's instincts were normal and feminine; in intelligence, in her way of looking at things, she was more like a man.
Girls with a strain of literary or artistic talent approach life
with the same impersonal interest as similarly gifted persons of
the opposite sex, but have less staying power."

Despite this unresolved problem, there are many fine passages
of great beauty and intelligence. The best of these, which
delineates with considerable ingenuity and skill the antagonistic
standpoint from which older and younger generations look on
love, and on life itself for that matter, would be better placed
in an essay than a novel, where it obtrudes on the reader's
attention, drawing him away not only from the narrative, but
from the characters themselves. But the young always fear
being misunderstood, which is partly the reason why they
seldom write masterpieces. Towards the close of this disserta-
tion on generations, a note of ill-concealed exasperation is injected into the writing. Kingsmill, metaphorically speaking,
grasps the reader by the lapel and shouts loudly into his ear
that intolerance should not be tolerated. It is all enlivening
and stimulating stuff this, but a moment later one is surprisingly
plunged back into the main flow of the narrative which, even
after rallying one's scattered faculties, reads like a different
book.

In *The Will to Love*, too, he defined for the first time the
frontiers of literary criticism and biography, past which he
would always seek to advance. "The brain," he wrote, "can
do no more than register the emotions of the heart. It cannot
divine the nature of noble emotion by hard thought." But the
artist, he felt, could recreate the impression of such emotion
in imaginative fiction, and so come "nearer to the essence of
life."

7

Switzerland Again

FROM 1921 UNTIL 1927 KINGSMILL, TOGETHER WITH HIS TWO
brothers Arnold and Brian, worked in their father's tourist
agency, Kingsmill spending most of this period at Lucerne in
Switzerland, a country which ever since childhood had held a
strong, dream-like appeal for him. About this time, too, the
various Lunn offices throughout Europe appear to have become
suddenly staffed with a number of his personal friends.

In 1922, as a representative of the family business, he co-
operated with a certain Frederick De Valda on a shortlived
scheme to find homes in France and other continental countries
for retired English officers and other persons of limited means.
De Valda's connection with the firm, to which he had been
enthusiastically introduced by Kingsmill, lasted altogether
about four months, cost them over three hundred pounds in
salaries, expenses, advertising and so forth, and succeeded in
assembling a total of nine would-be colonists, with seven of
whom an unfriendly correspondence was carried on for many
years afterwards. Kingsmill's activities in this affair had one
important result in providing him with material for his *W.J.*
and part of the background to *The Return of William Shakespeare,* in both of which De Valda appears under the name of
Melmoth—"a curiously intense man, with those large horn-
rimmed glasses, through which he projected so mesmeric a
glare."

It is important in view of later events to understand fully
Kingsmill's position during these years. He was given by his
father a very large salary indeed, about £2,000 a year, so that
he was troubled by no direct financial problems at all. In

return he and his family—his wife and their daughter, Kathleen—were, of course, entirely dependent upon Sir Henry Lunn, who always considered his sons to be largely irresponsible. Consequently Kingsmill developed little practical sense, while his father allowed him few interesting or responsible jobs and, as time went by, grew increasingly anxious over the size of the salary he was paying him. Sir Arnold Lunn was of the opinion that "Hugh was useless in winter, and did nothing in spring and summer," though Kingsmill rather unrealistically considered his brother to have doubtful and even sinister motives for expressing such a view. He himself was obviously of a different mind and, in Malcolm Muggeridge's words, "rather disliked being regarded as impractical, and a distinctly high note would come into his voice as he pointed out that during his time at Interlaken in charge of the Lunn office a record amount of business had been done there." Most probably his father's lack of regard for him considerably vexed Kingsmill, for he was always eager for other people's good opinion—even his family's.

Something of the individual nature of his efforts to become a successful member of a tourist agency can be gathered from a story he told Hesketh Pearson. One day when he was in his Lucerne office, one of the tourists, a stout middle-aged woman, came in. She had just returned from the Burgenstock, so she informed him, and had dropped her bag down the precipice at the top. It contained her passport, a spare set of false teeth and twenty-five pounds in English notes. Could Kingsmill do anything about this serious loss?

Warming to a task which promised more variety than the usual routine work such as translating German guide books and pamphlets into English, he set out for the Burgenstock the very next afternoon. The place he eventually selected for his descent, though not sheer, was steep, and the loose stones he dislodged with his exertions bounded out of sight in four or five leaps. Suddenly, just after three or four rocks had gone tumbling down in this fashion, a number of piercing shrieks sounded from below. Certain that he had knocked out, if not actually battered to death at least one sightseer, he continued his descent more carefully. But soon more rocks hurtled out of sight and more screams came from below. Collecting himself again Kingsmill proceeded with extreme gingerliness, feeling that the least he could do would be to collect any farewell messages from the victims below, should any of them still have breath left in their bodies.

Soon the path came into view, on which stood three girls, white and shaking. Kingsmill hurried towards them, to be bitterly upbraided by the most formidable of the three. His apologies composed them after a while, and they explained that they had been sitting on a bench a little way down the path, and were about to rise when the first consignment of rocks shot above their heads, missing them by a yard. Then, just when they had mustered enough courage to make a dash for it, the second lot shot over their heads. Hence the screams.

They soon made friends and Kingsmill took the three of them to tea at the Burgenstock Hotel. They were working girls and their names were Betty, Lily and Alice. The next day he sent them on the Rhone Glacier Motor Tour, and on a card he had from them on their return they wrote : *"Le temps était splendide, la compaignie charmante, et bien sûre que cette journée du 21 août 1923, n'a pas compté de petites filles plus heureuses que nous."*

The following week another employee went down the Burgenstock and rescued a bag containing a passport, a spare set of false teeth, and twenty-five pounds in English notes.

During these years in the family business, Kingsmill wrote two books, *The Dawn's Delay*, published at his own expense in 1924, and *Blondel*, which although completed some time earlier, was not published until 1927, when he had left the family business.

The Dawn's Delay is a collection of three short novels. Longest and most important of these is *W.J.*, the action of which takes place over the period of a week at a schloss near

Audernach in Southern Germany, and which attempts to show "a cross-grained genius in the society of ordinary persons." As an endeavour to convey the spirit of genius without lapsing into melodrama the story is wholly successful, and remains the finest piece of fiction which he ever wrote, being a small master-piece in its own right. Gleg, a man in his middle fifties, is the "W.J." of the title, having been given this nickname by the other paying guests at the schloss one evening when, coming down drunk to dinner, he informed all those present that he was a genius and had been engaged for thirty years in writing a masterpiece called *The Wandering Jew.*

The minor characters of this tale are brilliantly drawn, and their complex inter-relationship is surprisingly well handled with a mixture of humour, insight and sympathy. Their separ-ate and joint attitudes and reactions are entertainingly and exactly observed throughout : Fleet, the shrewd and sardonic journalist; Smith, the self-conscious nineteen-year-old boy in love with the housekeeper's younger sister; Miss Elizabeth Taylor, the nervous and romantic elderly spinster, author of *Mary: The Story of a Plain Woman;* Bull, the robust and pompous bluffer, Major Walden, conceited and stupid, with his wife who, like so many utterly bored people leading an empty existence, is a born trouble-maker. But above all these ordinary individuals towers the figure of "W.J." He is the humanist who has gone "rotten", who both envies and rebels against religion; he is the genius who has never come to terms with life, who has never yielded to those weaknesses, such as snobbery, which conciliate society. His faults instead are those which in their tangled co-existence turn back in on himself and conciliate no one—envy, lust, vanity and ambition. Longing for both power and love at the same time, he achieves neither, and, self-centered and isolated from his fellow beings, he rages against a life which once promised so much but which has finally given him so little. His magnificently written mono-logues to Smith, who temporarily ostracized from the society at the schloss for a breach of good manners, becomes for a time his disciple, give an added power and vigour to the story and display a nature which combines the frustrated potential of John Holms, with the force and drive of Frank Harris.

In the course of his talk to Smith, "W.J." outlines the scheme of his as yet incompleted masterpiece. He is at once attracted by Christ's inner tranquillity, which symbolizes to his imagination a capacity to transcend life, but two obstacles prevent him from following the Saviour. First, his own sense of vanity does not encourage him to identify himself with the materialistic failures to whom Christ's gospel is particularly addressed—an implied criticism of Christ's unequal sympathy which favours those who are rejected by the world and there-fore similar to himself. Secondly, and this is the essence of Kingsmill's argument, the isolation of Christ does not satisfy the spirit of the Jew. Led on by an ever unfulfilled promise of happiness, he is thirsty for life; he wants to experience as much of it as he can, with all its joys and tribulations. But Christ is not of this world. He remains always alone and remote, nourished by some far off and unknown source.

At the Crucifixion life triumphs over Christ, and the Jew kneels at his feet.

Beneath his sometimes automatic resentment against a life which eternally withholds its secret of happiness from him, he conceals a longing for human love which is exploited by some of the other guests at the schloss in order to hold him up to general ridicule. This feat is accomplished with the aid of a malicious and grotesque scheme devised by a sly eighteen-year-old girl, soured by her own failure to have a love-affair. This girl plays the leading role in the plan while a number of the others act as audience.

The form of *W.J.* has struck some critics as strange, even unintelligible. But if a work possesses both force and sincerity, as *W.J.* does, it creates its own most suitable form. The appar-ent strangeness is nothing more or less than the originality that proceeds from genuine emotion combined with intellect. The story is written with great economy and power. Nothing which is irrelevant is given place; none of the guests speak or act out of character. Altogether it is a remarkable achievement with which Kingsmill himself was well pleased, telling Hesketh Pearson that he would rather have written it than Balzac's *Curé de Tours,* and adding, "it's more or less my compendium of life."

The second of the three short novels, *The End of the World,* which was also published separately in *Georgian Stories 1925,* is scarcely less good than *W.J.* The two main figures in this story are Glayde, who is Kingsmill's portrait of Alec Waugh, an Oxford history don who longs to be a man of action, a lean, nervous and at times irritable person, disillusioned in himself and possessing an insatiable hunger for a life which is beyond his reach; and Polmont, Kingsmill's most successful and complete portrayal of himself in fiction—a man of leisure by temperament, ample, rotund, bulky, of a humorous disposition, breezy and exuberant, and touched by the poetry of life, who, for his own amusement, sketches literary caricatures in the manner of Max Beerbohm.

These two men meet for a day at a small village, Azay-le-Rideau, in Touraine, where Glayde, with the passion of final regret, eagerly convinces Polmont of a prognostication made by a certain Professor Weedon, an eccentric astronomer at Oxford, that a comet is to collide with the earth that very night. Polmont is impressed by his companion's obvious sincerity and his personal knowledge of Weedon—for, as he ruefully remarks, "Noah's ark must have been a stock joke in the neighbourhood until the barometer began to fall."

The two men are naturally well read, and much of their dialogue is studded with literary idioms, quotations and allusions both ingenious and witty, ranging from Descartes to Thomas Aquinas. These literary discussions and parodies, which in Kingsmill correspond to Polmont's caricatures, are in places over-indulged and are not always worked sufficiently closely and unobtrusively into the main narrative sequence.

Apart from this common interest in literature Polmont and

Glayde, while possessing some feelings of mutual sympathy, do not altogether approve of one another. What affection they do hold for each other is dictated more by their common predicament than by any deep similarity of temperament. Both of them, moreover, are somewhat sensitive. "These history dons," Polmont reflects sourly to himself, "are all alike. They write a chapter on Napoleon Bonaparte for the Cambridge Modern History and spend the rest of their lives failing to intimidate railway porters and apologizing to waiters whom they've insulted." And Glayde reproves Polmont sternly at another point with, "You are quite amusing, Polmont, but life is something more than a mere occasion for verbal fireworks. Great literature is the child of great action."

Both the resemblance and incompatibility of the two men are sympathetically revealed and subtly brought out early on in the story when they are visiting a nearby château together.

" 'Azay-le-Rideau!' he [Polmont] murmured, 'Azay-le-Rideau!' The sweet name of the little village enchanted him. His heart yearned over its inhabitants. . . . His companion sighed.

" 'What, sagging, man?' boomed Polmont. 'Look around you! Pluck up your heart. Rich prose, Glayde, rich prose, these cobbled streets, snug houses, plentiful food, good wine, and love and love! Exuberance and strength! And the gently flowing Indre, Glayde—there's poetry; and the bright sky beyond the line of that slope. There lies the South—blue hills and tiny horses bearing tiny cavaliers past toy castles. Isn't there a memory that includes all memories? Is it mere years and facts we recall? Do we not remember centuries and the dreams of dead men? Ah! The château! How it all comes back to me! Out into the world beyond these trees, Glayde! High politics, bloody slaughter : then home again, white clinging arms, rest after long war. Oh Glayde! Glayde! Glayde!'

" 'Do you think,' said Glayde intensely . . . 'that I can't feel romance, too? Do you think a don isn't human? . . .'

". . . (they) walked towards the château in silence.

" 'Polmont,' Glayde quavered suddenly, 'don't you think that they at any rate must have been happy, those old kings and their mistresses, in this charming place? It's as beautiful as a dream, these turrets and spires, this stream wandering here and there, the grass, the trees. Perhaps after all its been worth while, I mean this world, life generally, simply because these wonderful creatures lived here and were happy, happy.

" 'And yet,' he added, after a pause, 'I dare say this notion of their happiness is merely another illusion, due perhaps to my having drunk somewhat freely, that is for me. I dare say they were as miserable as the rest of us. It's a poor world, Polmont'."

It is not the business of a poet, Wordsworth has said, to make an inventory of nature, and in the above passage there is consequently no long-winded, accurate or formalized description of the scenery, but a personal and private impression communicated to the reader, a vision pregnant with lyricism, a glimpse of nature, a fragrance of the place itself exuded in only a few words. And like most great writing, which is at once poetic and flexible, it all appears so easy, effortless and simple that one is surprised by the depth and force liberated by such a clear, uncomplicated prose style.

In one of the most inspired passages from the story, Kingsmill communicates his own vibrant stereoscopic vision of life, which was to reappear in various forms in many of his later writings. But of all his vivid evocations none is perhaps so moving, so intense and so natural as the first one. "Mysticism," he wrote many years later, "is the intuition of a harmony which envelopes but does not penetrate this life, and which can be apprehended but not completely possessed," and his mystical view of life as given in *The End of the World* is illumined by obvious personal experience. There is no pedantry in the following passage, no attempt to substitute erudition for insight or a lifeless terminology for living words. The writing is free, the effect magical.

"From his bedroom window Polmont gazed at the statue of Balzac, half hidden by the chestnut trees, and groaned :

" 'Well, and what then is the meaning of it all ? Shakespeare says that the world itself is a dream, and that we shall wake out of life into nothingness. But I say we shall wake into life. The world is real—houses and trees, men and women, motor buses and the moaning sea. But we have fallen asleep, and all these things, these simple and reasonable things, have been confused for us. But now the dream draws to its close, and we shall awake and smile at the perplexity and confusion that sleep has shed upon the world. Once more we shall see life as, even in this dream, I saw it a few minutes ago, the cab-horse and the stars, the chestnut trees and eternity, the great and the little, all parts of a self-explained and satisfying whole. My friends, be patient'."

"There are a great many writers," William Gerhardi remarked on a B.B.C. talk devoted to this book, "who write of mysticism without being able to evoke the experience they are trying to describe, but when Kingsmill . . . writes these words he uses none of the terms of mystical philosophers, but through the miracle of poetry he evokes the very feeling they have failed to beguile with definitions . . . the focus is new, and the familiar world stands, fresh and new, as though preening itself on its many-sided facets and aspects we had not suspected, until the new illumination opened our eyes."

The End of the World is the first piece of writing in which a number of words of Kingsmill's own invention make their appearance. The most celebrated of these is "Dawnist"—a political leftist with a propensity always to see the new dawn. The word is intended to demolish by implication an illusion, for, as Malcolm Muggeridge wrote, "just by that word he showed how absurd it all was, leading in its inevitable way to another afternoon and another evening." A number of years later Kingsmill wrote a long chapter, "Dawnism," in his biographical study of Matthew Arnold. "Dawnism," he explained, "or heralding the dawn of a new world . . . an excited anticipation that some form of collective action is about to solve all the troubles of the individual is an intermittent but apparently incurable malady of mankind.

"The essence of dawnism being to escape from the sphere of the individual into an ideal collective sphere, dawnism is most intense where the conditions of life are least favourable to the individual."

Later still, in *The Poisoned Crown,* he gave his most succinct definition of dawnism or utopianism as "the transference to society of the individual's disappointed expectation of personal happiness."

A politician called Victor Stubbs is the central character in the third and last of his short novels, *The Disintegration of a Politician.* Destined first to be the victim of his own carelessness which leads on to mental instability, immediate retirement from public life and finally premature death, this illfated hero is given the surname of the author of those lengthy investigations into the Anglo-Saxons which Kingsmill was obliged to study at Oxford. But after only a few pages it becomes clear that Stubbs is in fact a very clever and witty portrayal of Asquith, containing a deft parody on his manner of speech-making, and it may well be that, by giving him the surname of a scholar, Kingsmill was alluding to those academic qualities in the late Prime Minister which were to be so accentuated in his obituary notices some four years later, to the vexation of several of his admirers.

The Disintegration of a Politician opens in October 1920. Stubbs, coming down to breakfast, trips and strikes the third

stair from the bottom with his right temple, an accident which
gives rise to the ensuing story. This device of a blow on the
head, used to give added impetus and penetration to a novel,
appealed very greatly to Kingsmill, who used it again later in
The Fall. By such a means he endeavoured to pierce the everyday superficialities of life and reveal that part which remains
unspoken, even unknown, during most of our lives. On the
technical side this method helped him to overcome the difficulty
of a lyric poet writing novels—that of dealing adequately with
everyday routine. In *The Disintegration of a Politician,* where
the writing is permeated with humour, where there exists
detachment and even pathos, such a device is justified by its
success. But in *The Fall*, where the visions are more elegant
and elaborate, where the super-consciousness does not transcend the personal and egotistical element in man, this technique is ineffective and unsatisfactory, for great skill and
economy of language are necessary to carry it off. In this case,
the everyday utterances of sophisticated sentiments are incon-
gruously funny when set against Stubbs's unpractised, half-
incoherent and disjointed expressions of genuine emotion,
brought suddenly to the surface by his illness. It is with considerable skill that Kingsmill makes the usual behaviour of the
other persons rather than the extraordinary behaviour of Stubbs
seem ludicrous and inadequate. All through the story political
and social life is contrasted with real life. To take one example,
there is a play on the meaning of vision—political vision and
mystical vision.

"The appointment as Minister of Education of a man
whose life had been spent in educational work was quoted
at the time as an instance of the Premier's happy audacity.
"Vision! That at any rate could not be denied the
man."

So much for political vision : Stubbs's vision is less adept.
His wife, going up to his bedroom, is shocked as she enters the
room to find him emerging suddenly from beneath the bed.

" 'Good God, Victor !' she cried.

"Stubbs clambered into bed, looking rather foolish.

" 'Crocks of gold,' he murmured. . . . 'I was hunting for it . . . symbol of happiness.'

"There was a bump on his forehead. He passed his hand over it ruefully.

" 'Just like life !' he murmured. 'Life all over !'

"It was clear that his researches had not been without incident—incident susceptible, it would seem, to symbolic interpretation."

Mrs. Stubbs hurries off to fetch the doctor while Stubbs himself, taking advantage of his wife's absence, jumps out of bed, dresses quickly and makes good his escape from the house. As if in a nightmare, he wanders along the empty soundless streets, and all at once hears the clop-clop of horses' hoofs approaching. They beat like some mocking tattoo upon his ears, an echo of the ordered, vain progress of his own life. He turns, and sees a hansom-cab in which sits his youthful self, cold-eyed and preoccupied. Horror rises up inside him, and, almost unconscious, he lets out a scream. Borne up by this emotional pressure, the mystical vision of life returns.

"An old man with straggling grey hair—he saw himself clearly, as though he were outside his body—stumbling through the chaos of a disintegrating world. How firm an outline the world had presented to that young fellow in the cab !

"High above North London a mountain towered, on whose western flank there rested a glow, as from a central sun shining even to the ends of the universe. He stretched out his arms to the fading glow, but glow and mountain dissolved in the night."

There are fewer literary allusions in this story than in *The End of the World*. Even so, half a page is expanded at one stage for no other reason than to include the sentence : "I

prefer the Biblical exegis of Dostoievsky's fallen women to the
mother solicitude of Arnold Bennett's and the commercial integrity of Shaw's." Apart from this, the story contains a parody
of W. E. Henley, and one of Herbert Trench's poem *Apollo
and the Seaman,* in which it may not be too fanciful to suppose Kingsmill forecast his own future :

" 'Faster ! Faster ! Stick it out. No good ! Poor old nag !
Poor old nag !' he muttered to himself, turning something
over in his mind, then declaimed with slow pathos :

> " 'I heard men crying in the streets
> That the horse my shirt was on,
> The great horse Sprig o' Rosemary
> Had finished last but one.

" 'Last but one ! To me that is even better than last,
more humiliating. The great horse Sprig o' Rosemary !
And victory had seemed so sure. The pity of it ! Oh life,
oh life !' "

The Dawn's Delay is the strongest fiction Kingsmill was ever
to write. His longing for happiness is most movingly expressed,
too, in these stories, for it does not overflow into sentimentality,
but is checked by experience, pathos, stamina—"My friends,
be patient !" In such passages his whole character is revealed;
his open natural temperament attuned for present happiness
in conflict with his narrow early upbringing which trained him
for endurance and endeavour without the promise of earthly
reward. His longer novels contain pages of great beauty, but
they are interspersed with other pages which fall far below his
best, while *The Dawn's Delay* possesses an aura which remains
with one long after finishing the book; for all three stories con-
form to the precept laid down by Coleridge that "nothing can
permanently please which does not contain in itself the reason
why it is so, and not otherwise."

8

Made on Earth

IN APRIL 1927, SHORTLY AFTER HIS WIFE HAD RETURNED FROM
Switzerland to England, Kingsmill met a girl at Wengen with
whom he fell more deeply in love than ever before or afterwards. Though he was later to become disillusioned in Gladys,
the girl who inspired these feelings, he always looked upon his
love for her as the deepest emotional experience of his life.
With her he hoped to recapture that perfect, unmixed adora-
tion which all imaginative persons feel in their early years.
This hope, fed on his yearning for happiness and nourished
by his being back once more in the land of his childhood,
swelled up and suffocated the powers of reason within him
which knew from experience that such adult feelings are permanently unobtainable in this life. The retrospective impression
which this "platonic idyll" (to use Sir Arnold Lunn's words)
left with him was intensified by its short duration. These days
were the most agonizing but wonderful in his life; he did not
know how much longer he could stand the strain and thought
that he would go completely to pieces; but the wonder was
well worth the agony. "Life has no value," he wrote to Hesketh Pearson, "except the inestimable value of a few immortal
hours, and one must endure the rest for their sake."

For some time even before this his marriage had not been
working out with conspicuous success. His first wife was not the
sort of woman he should ever have married, distrusting intel-
lectuals and being of an extremely domineering disposition. But
Kingsmill was not over fond of resisting temptation where
women were concerned and always fell very easily in love.
While in love, he seemed to exist under a spell which mes-

merized him and completely distorted his usually clear vision—
an effect which is reproduced in some of his fiction. When in
due course his normal mental faculties were restored to him,
he would hold "an affectionate disdain of women in general,"
and it was to his literary men-friends that he would turn for
intellectual nourishment. Thus he created for himself a type of
double life, interposing an artificial barrier between the domestic side of his existence, and the intellectual. This proved a far
from practical arrangement, disconcerting his friends, dis-
satisfying his wife and eventually disturbing himself. Malcolm
Muggeridge, who first met Kingsmill in 1930, noticed that
"one always had a queer feeling when one said goodbye to him
that he was, as it were, going off into the unknown. There was
no continuity, or so it seemed. . . . One saw him and then he
was gone, and until one saw him again it was a sort of blank."
William Gerhardi, who met him a few years earlier, and made
him the main character in his novel *Pending Heaven,* noted
also that his "tricks of suddenly running away without telling
where or why—a habit acquired in evading an exacting wife
in the course of a long and unsuccessful married life—displayed
themselves unaccountably and, as it appeared to his associates,
unnecessarily. . . ."

Kingsmill also liked to sub-divide his friends into small compartments of their own and it was his habit to resemble temporarily any friend to whom he was writing or talking. Thus
he was often tortuously hesitant in the company of John
Holms; with Hesketh Pearson he was inclined to be more
exuberantly cheerful. In the presence of William Gerhardi he
could be sophisticated and witty. Each of his friends possessed
some special appeal for him which bordered at times upon a
duty which they were in honour bound to accord him. Holms's
duty, as we have already seen, was to maintain Kingsmill's
confidence by his own greater lack of confidence, coupled with
fierce and repeated avowals of enthusiasm in the supremacy
of his fiction. After Holms's death the task of praising his
novels was delegated to Gerhardi, who interspersed it some-

what erratically with a greater celebration of his own fiction.
But with him Kingsmill could also nourish his feelings of
mysticism. With Hesketh Pearson the appeal was probably a
wide and common appreciation of English literature combined
with a sympathetic but vigorous good humour which evap-
orated the burden of endless financial difficulties which beset
him. In Malcolm Muggeridge, whose *Samuel Butler* had been
greatly influenced by *After Puritanism,* he saw perhaps his one
and only disciple, a man with an alert, entertaining and intriguing mind.

Throughout the uneasy years of his first marriage Kingsmill
became far too servile under his wife's demanding personality.
Possibly, had his whole being been bound up with this union
and his attitude been in consequence less apathetic and passive,
he might have exerted himself early on and not allowed
matters to reach the pitch they did. But equally, there would
seem to be little object in his doing so if it was merely to conceal their essential differences and to prolong such an ill-suited
match.

But although husband and wife had worn out their lives in
altercation since the earliest days of their marriage, the rift
between them was not opened up inseparably until the beginning of 1927, when Eileen found the typescript of *Blondel,* a
novel based on a love-affair Kingsmill had had in his 'teens
with an Irish cousin. Under a barrage of questions and plead-
ings he eventually agreed to destroy the manuscript—a promise
which fortunately he did not honour.

Immediately after his experience in Switzerland, Kingsmill
asked his wife for a divorce; she refused and informed Sir
Henry Lunn; and a long and acrimonious correspondence between father and son ensued. Sir Henry pointed out that if
Kingsmill wished to obtain a divorce, he must be prepared
to give up his job, since he could not as a divorced man continue to remain in a key position with a Free Church Touring
Guild. In fairness to him it must be admitted that the position
as viewed from his standpoint was tricky. Previously, another

member of the staff had been asked to resign when divorced and there was no question of according his son preferential treatment in such conspicuous circumstances. Kingsmill's letters to his father did nothing to conciliate Sir Henry who, according to his own standards, acted perfectly correctly. But according to other, more intelligent standards, he may be said to have acted ruthlessly, for while he supported Kingsmill's wife and daughter, he saw to it that Kingsmill himself was removed from his job and given almost no money whatever. At first he warned him to return to Eileen and patch up the marriage, and his general attitude to Kingsmill furnishes just one more instance of the fact that the ordinary commonsense advice of an experienced man of the world is almost always out of place where a man of genius is involved. Undoubtedly Kingsmill was unduly harsh and bitter in his letters to Sir Henry and in later years came to regret their tone. His brother, Arnold, seems for the most part to have supported their father during this controversial period and maintains that Kingsmill was treated justly. For years he had been paid more than his worth, and for years he must have known what effect a divorce would have on his position. He had only himself to blame for what happened. Kingsmill, on his side, blamed Sir Henry for having kept his children dependent on him to such an extent that, as a man of thirty-eight, he himself was not allowed to manage his personal affairs in private, but must be penalized and even pauperized for taking the only sensible course open to him. "After depriving me of the means to support my wife and child," he wrote to Sir Henry, "you make a merit of supporting them yourself. In other words, after kicking me into the gutter, you pride yourself on not sending my wife and child after me."

Sir Henry Lunn should never have been in the position to send Kingsmill or any of his family into the gutter by this time. But the blame does not rest entirely with him. As in his marriage, Kingsmill displayed not endurance but weakness in permitting a state of affairs to build up which was entirely inap-

propriate and which could only be demolished by a crisis. He
was fully aware of his status in the family business, but was
prepared to ignore its more unpleasant aspects for the sum of
£2,000 a year.

Kingsmill's nerves had been strained to snapping point
during May 1927 when the girl for whom he was prepared to
give up his job, renounce his family and leave his wife decided,
after due deliberation, to reject him in favour of her wealthy
guardian who had threatened to cut her off without any money
if she was to leave him. He was now in a state easily to be
provoked into indiscretion, and near to the complete collapse
which finally overtook him some weeks later. In June he travelled from Switzerland to talk over the question of divorce with
his wife and his father. Later the same month he returned from
London to Lucerne with Sir Henry's promise that his future
relations with Eileen would not be raised for four months, by
which time he would be in a calmer, more balanced frame of
mind to reach a decision. Sir Henry furthermore promised
Kingsmill that his wife would remain in England during this
time.

The day after his return to Switzerland he dined with his
brother Arnold at Grindelwald, and during the course of their
dinner Eileen, who had followed him out there again, rang
up. It transpired that she had been in touch with Arnold and
his wife for some time and that her return had been privately
arranged between them. Kingsmill then lost his temper and
stated, perhaps unwisely, that if he was to be persecuted in
such a manner, then he would leave the business.

Two days later, after he had returned to Lucerne, he received
two letters from Arnold passing on an ultimatum from his
father that if he did not resume relations with Eileen in the
autumn, he would be turned out of the business. On the evening of this day, when Kingsmill returned to his room he found
Eileen waiting for him there. Arnold and his wife had evidently
seen fit to bring her to Lucerne and deposit her in Kingsmill's
room that afternoon, before retiring themselves to a nearby

hotel to await the consequences of their action. Whether their
motives in performing this somewhat unlikely feat were due
to muddled altruism, or whether, as Kingsmill later suspected,
they were fully realized by the result produced, cannot be ascertained now. But "the next day," Kingsmill recounts, "I left
Lucerne and the business, feeling that anything was preferable
to four months' rest diversified by such ingenuity in persecuting
me as had been exhibited within four days." The note of martyrdom in this sentence is well balanced by Arnold's incredu-
lous indifference. "In the summer," he wrote, "Hugh walked
out of the Lucerne office, of which he was the manager, and
left no address . . . we immediately appointed a member of the
staff who was more efficient than Hugh at less than half his
salary."

Sir Henry Lunn was hot in condemning Kingsmill to others,
but seems somewhat more apprehensive when embarking on a
more direct approach, as if fearing to provoke his son into further temperamental indiscretions. Kingsmill's bitter and at
times unreasonable letters on the subject of money in the following few years, during which time he was constantly over-
drawn at the bank, are nicely corrected by his father's vague
evasiveness. On subjects other than finance though, Sir Henry
could display considerable alarm. In May 1930, some three
years after Kingsmill had left both his wife and the business,
and was lying in a Birmingham hospital recovering from a
minor operation, he received a telegram from his father. Assum-
ing that the text would convey parental relief at his recovery,
he opened it without undue excitement. It ran : *"Your doctor
knows my Birmingham cousins if they call speak carefully
about Eileen."*

Kingsmill's divorce was arranged some while after he left
the family business, and his wife afterwards married again, this
time to a Belgian with whom she spent the Second World War
in occupied Belgium. Brian Lunn's marriage also collapsed,
whereupon he was removed from the tourist agency in similar
fashion to his brother. His wife had left him for a Jugoslav,

and at the end of the war both she and Eileen reappeared safe
and sound in their respective countries. "The sea gives up its
dead," Kingsmill murmured, "and liberated Europe gives up
its Mrs. Lunns."

9

"Blondel"

DURING THESE UPHEAVALS KINGSMILL'S SECOND NOVEL, *Blondel* was published. He had started this novel early in 1925, and the love-affair which he experienced in Switzerland, gave a fresh impetus to the book which had been laid temporarily aside after his wife's complaints, and he rewrote the last third of it in three days—fourteen continuous hours on the first two days, and nine on the third. The sudden pulsing energy which possessed him at this time flows through every line, and one is led racing through the story, page after page. "Nothing but Titanic enterprise can satisfy the enormous energy that continues to churn up in me," he wrote to Hesketh Pearson on completing the novel, "Send me a stud of elephants to massage. That will occupy me before breakfast."

The theme of *Blondel* is the falsity of the romantic view of life, and the treatment is similar to that used in an early essay called *The Journey*, which had been published in 1912. But the novel is far more succinct and its theme is not confused, as the essay is, with a personal feeling of regret. Placed in the period of Richard Coeur de Lion, so as to achieve the objectivity he found so difficult to maintain in his fiction, it opens with Blondel, an egotistical wandering minstrel, taking leave of a party of tumblers one of whom, a pretty girl named Suzanne, is in love with him. Musing to himself as to why he should be leaving such charming company, he comes to the conclusion that "life held something more for him than the faithful love of a humble girl, however pretty."

At the castle of Gruyères where he presently arrives, Blondel notices a bewitching young girl, who seems indifferent to the

glances of all the men around her. On inquiry he finds out
that her name is Anne, and that she is an armourer's orphan.

The following day they are expelled from Gruyères together
after Blondel has helped Anne to repel an assault by the Count
in the grounds of the castle. Anne determines at once to travel
to the Holy Land, and to command respect and protection for
herself on the way she gives it out that she has made a vow to
arrive there "a virgin unspotted." Her real desire in going is to
see that mighty warrior Richard Coeur de Lion, stories of
whose superb physique, extraordinary prowess and triumphant
crusades have thrilled her daily from afar. She easily persuades
Blondel to help her to reach the Holy Land, for though he
disapproves of the venture he is powerless to resist any request
she makes of him. And so they journey on, she remaining with
him so that he can assist and protect her, he fatally attracted to
her through a mixture of vanity and desire. Their short periods
of precarious harmony, the perpetual anguish of Blondel, his
sudden wild hopes and the spasms of irritation of Anne, the
imperceptible changes in their relationship as they wander onwards over the beautiful country and across the sea, all these
are marvellously captured, giving the journey a poetic, almost
magical quality. Chapter after chapter palpitates with a great
spirit of vitality and high intensity of feeling, and in Blondel's
dog-like devotion through the blows, contempt, ingratitude and
humiliation he receives as the journey proceeds, we can easily
see Kingsmill's own complete subservience to the woman of
the moment. It was this aspect of the book which made Gerald
Gould write that it was a greater novel than *Manon Lescaut*.
Certainly it is the most easily readable of all Kingsmill's novels,
but since the narrative seldom reaches complete detachment,
we are permitted little humour. Thus, although the story is told
in the third person throughout, we see Anne only through
Blondel's eyes as a perfect, idealized, but lifeless statuette. As
a symbol of life she is eternally beyond Blondel's reach in all
their wanderings together, and, at the end, as a symbol of
death, she is still out of reach. She signifies a release from the

afflictions of this world, which all men strain for, but which few even momentarily attain.

"The advantage to a writer of setting his theme in a past age," Kingsmill wrote about this time, "or in a foreign country, is simply that he can see it better at a distance, and treat it more freely." But in *Blondel* the only figures to be portrayed with clarity and detachment are the purely historical ones, such as Richard, the others being as much of this century as of any other, and only moving against a medieval background. Had his treatment been less direct it might have been more objective, but though he may be said to have had a sense of history, Kingsmill was no historian, and *Blondel* is not an historical novel. He was primarily concerned with that part of the individual which transcends the bounds of time and place, while history on the other hand he defined as the sorry record "of the convulsions by the grown man's efforts to find in company with others what he had failed to find alone as child and boy and youth." Contrasting fiction with historical portraiture, he once said, "In fiction one can develop a hint in imaginary scenes thus vitalizing the portrait beyond the reach of mere statements."

After much suffering, exhaustion and disillusionment began to weigh on Blondel towards the end of his pilgrimage with Anne, and in weariness he sings :

> "What day will see my journey done?
>   On what high noontide shall I creep
> Out of the dust, out of the sun,
>   Into a little field to sleep?
>
> The clear light at the horizon's bound
>   Still fled me as I hastened on.
> Sharp flints and sullen folks I found
>   Where yesterday the clear light shone."

When at long last they reach the Holy Land and meet up with Richard, a truce has been declared, much to the astonished

disgust of the would-be crusaders with whom Blondel and
Anne had travelled the last stage of their voyage. There is a
good picture of the vain, immature and conceited swashbuckler,
Richard, whose most permanent feeling is that he, above all
others, has been hard done by in life. Cantankerous and en-
feebled, with his thin and straggling hair he is hardly the
golden curled warrior whose splendid reputation had spread
to Gruyères. But just as Blondel still worships Anne after all
her savage and inhuman treatment of him, so Anne herself sees
Richard not as the man he is, but as the mythical and romantic
figure which legend has painted him. Shortly after her arrival
in the Holy Land, and in the presence of Richard she comes
to realize that her original vow of virginity has been finally
fulfilled and need not be extended over her stay there. Blondel,
who has fallen out of favour with Richard for criticizing his
verses, surprises these two alone in a tent, for which trouble he
is rewarded with a severe thrashing which Richard forces Anne
to administer. Richard himself, disquieted with the whole
episode, then promptly banishes Anne from his presence, never
to return.

Anne, a little later on, is killed by a man to whom she
promised she would shortly return back at Gruyères, while
Blondel, recovering after a week of delirium and now having
lost for ever the infinite expectancy of youth with which he
began his adventure, finds his exhausted disillusion liberated in
verse :

"Once your disquietude was mine,
    O millions of the unhappy earth,
But now the coils of sense untwine,
    That caught and clasped me at my birth.

Life has confused and troubled me
    I have not found the thing I sought.
Farewell harsh land and bitter sea,
    And farewell, love, and farewell, thought."

In a short "Conclusion" at the end of *Blondel*, Kingsmill goes on to stress that despite these lessons which individuals force upon themselves, the romantic view of life will always persist; buoyant and unabashed among so many young, licking its wounds in concealment but ready to spring out once more at the first sign of hope renewed in the breasts of the older and more mature.

10

"Matthew Arnold"

AFTER LEAVING LUCERNE KINGSMILL DRIFTED AROUND FRANCE, alone and completely cut off from his family. His nervous tension and sense of loneliness were now very great, and his morale sank lower than ever before or afterwards. Life was devoid of all pleasure or encouragement during these months, and the solitude which overflowed in a number of letters to his friends, grew increasingly oppressive. "The loneliness takes it out of one," he confided, "and I am out of bed twice a night sleep-walking. In fact the nights are very bad indeed." He hoped that his isolation would cure his restless mania, and not long after leaving Lucerne he drew up a list of all the places to which he had been during the previous four months, together with the number of nights he had spent there. It makes curious reading :

Hastings	37 nights		
Lucerne	28 nights	Leeds	
London	12 nights	Windermere	
In train	9 nights	Keswick	
Geneva	7 nights	Leicester	
Mentone	4 nights	Wigan	
Lausanne	3 nights	Berne	1 night
Bath	3 nights	Cassis	
Grindelwald	2 nights	Marseilles	
Paris	2 nights	Cette	
Toulon	2 nights	Nantes	
Montreux	2 nights	Quiberon	
Chesham	2 nights		

"Would Odysseus," he asked, "have covered so much ground if he had been a bachelor?" And with another half rueful recollection of the past, he remarked, "A lonely bed, once the great object of all my hopes, is now impossibly revolting to me."

Some weeks later he arrived in Nice where John Holms, who met him there, was startled by the unrealistic scale at which he appeared determined to carry on living. It was as if he did not fully comprehend that his large salary had been finally cut off, that he was no longer a comparatively rich man. After leaving Nice he went on to Toulon where, for the first time, he met William Gerhardi. In his *Memoirs of a Polyglot*, Gerhardi has given an account of the vivid impression which this meeting with Kingsmill made on him. The first thing he noticed was Kingsmill's striking similarity to Polmont, the hero, of his short novel, *The End of the World*.

> "He strode capaciously, his arms swinging to and fro; he walked with a sudden burst of initiative as who might say : 'Come on now, old man, we'll show 'em what we can do !'
>
> "We boarded an open tram, the clanking familiarity of which palled on me. But I noticed that Kingsmill sat beside me with a wondrous smile; and when an Italian peasant passed us in his donkey-cart Hugh murmured beatifically, and when, screeching, we curved into Toulon past a slatternly old woman who was hanging out her washing, Hugh, like Polmont, waved his hand to her, and when she smiled he said these folk of the Midi were hard to beat for sheer excellence of human nature. . . .
>
> "There was about him, I noticed at once, a certain ebullient naturalness, a glint about the eyes . . . which denotes a kind of gaiety of spirit, the real name for which is genius, and which intoxicates one."

The day after Kingsmill arrived at Toulon, Gerhardi called at his hotel only to be informed that he had embarked some hours ago an a walking-tour across France, without leaving any address—a characteristically furtive disappearance.

Although he had so surprised John Holms at Nice with his apparent ignorance of his own financial position and of what it entailed, he soon started work and by February 1928 he was living at St. Tropez with a girl whom he described as "the most surprising, vital and devastating person I have ever met," and, between exchanging letters of violent financial disagreement with his father, was engaged on a study of Matthew Arnold. From this time onwards, up to the end of his life, he was never free from an acute shortage of money. Harassed continually, and harassing others, he was at times down to his last half-crown, sometimes indeed was unable to afford a meal until he had sold his review copies of books to a friendly bookseller at two-thirds the published price.

"Up to that time (1927)," he wrote, "my net profit on my books (two novels and a volume of short stories) was slightly under three pounds, but they had been well received, and my literary agent told me that he could get me an advance both in England and in the States on a biography of Matthew Arnold. So I felt there was nothing for it except to include fiction, for the time being, among the things, persons and places from which I was parting, and to try my hand at a form of writing by which, as it approached reality through the individual, I had always been attracted."

Matthew Arnold, whose "express wish" it was, as George Russell tells us, "that he might *not* be made the subject of a biography," was an unfortunate first choice. The book, when it came out, was reviewed in some papers with almost hysterical hostility, the fact that Kingsmill had referred to his subject as "Matt" throughout suggesting not that his treatment was fundamentally sympathetic, but rather that he should never have been entrusted with such a task in the first place. He became greatly incensed with this criticism, writing letters to a number of periodicals pointing out that he was perfectly entitled to refer to his subject in this abbreviated if rather

familar fashion. The only critic who appears to have met with
his wholehearted approval was Louis Wilkinson's wife, who,
with delicate feminine tact, applied balm to the wound, almost
suggesting that she would have been hurt if he had not called
Arnold "Matt", and that to have called him anything else
would have displayed a bluntness of taste which she had confidently and, as it turned out correctly, divined the impossibility
of his displaying. " 'Matt' has fallen completely flat," he complained to her, "or shall we say Matthew has fallen completely
flathew."

The writing in this biography is informal, fresh and lively,
the theme illustrating "the collapse of a poet into a prophet."
What so scandalized some readers above all else, was the unabashed statement that Marguerite of the poems was a real
woman with whom "Matt" had had a love-affair. Not content with this, Kingsmill proceeded sternly to reprimand
"Matt" for having left the girl due to a fear of his family's
regard for social considerations. "The reward for renunciation," he wrote, "is some good greater than the thing re-
nounced. To renounce with no vision of such good, from fear
or in automatic obedience to some formula, is to weaken
the springs of life, and to diminish the soul's resistance to this
world."

Kingsmill treated Arnold as "half a don and half a genius."
But by following up his over hasty tributes to the genius with
lengthy and enthusiastic passages of condenmation against the
don he provoked to anger those reviewers who were all don
and no genius. To read a few of their articles one would not
imagine that Kingsmill had ever observed Arnold's fine elegaic
tenderness or noted with sympathy that appealing desire of his
for a deeper and more simple state of human happiness than
his character, together with the circumstances created by
his character, allowed him to enjoy. But without doubt Kingsmill's treatment contains a disproportionate degree of censure,
which, even allowing for the inference that much of the blame
was intended as a type of back-handed compliment to Arnold,

implying that he had it in him to do better, nevertheless gives an unbalanced total impression of him by the end of the book. Kingsmill's approach to a biographical subject was always personal and original, but in this case much of his anger against Sir Henry Lunn was diverted on to poor Arnold. In dealing with Arnold's love for Marguerite, Kingsmill almost certainly had at the back of his mind his own recent love-affair in Switzerland. Arnold's decision to renounce Marguerite was incompatible with Kingsmill's abandonment of position and affluence, and consequently he saw Dr. Arnold's relationship to Matthew Arnold in the same light as Sir Henry Lunn's to himself. Matthew Arnold's eventual submission to the influence of paternal Victorianism, thus ran directly contrary to his own lifelong determination to escape completely from Puritanism into happiness. Since this struggle had reached a climax so recently, it is perhaps not surprising that there is a strong personal flavour to the book. He is unfair to Arnold in giving no indication of the complex difficulties attached to shaking off the effects of early environment, and by over-simplifying this issue he creates the impression that Arnold was faced with a single cut-and-dried decision which he bungled inconceivably.

As always while engaged on writing a book, Kingsmill was highly optimistic about its prospects. "I don't think I could have had a subject more suited to the circumstances in which I wrote it," he said. His publishers were less wholehearted in their enthusiasm and wanted him to tone down some of his quips, such as "Oscar Wilde's aesthetic movement, whose frontal attack on British Philistinism was itself surprised in its undefended rear by the alert officers of the law," or "Arnold would shrink from the picture of a well-to-do dissenting trades-man on his second nuptial night, joining in prayer with his ex-sister-in-law, before availing himself of the renewed mercies vouchsafed him by the Almighty."

"Surely these days," he commented, "one can print this sort of thing. I am going to contest every criticism." But later he modified this intention to the extent of revising several sections and rewriting the whole of the introduction. It is surprising that he was able to inject such gaiety and wit into the book at any stage. At first many people had condemned the idea of his writing on Arnold, and Kingsmill himself became increasingly bored by Arnold's letters. Finally he decided to write an introduction setting forth the difficulties he had encountered, but this idea was soon supplanted by another one, that of writing not a straight introduction but a full-length diary in which he could treat Arnold more freely and imaginatively. In this form, he decided, he could give his own idea of the Swiss love-affair, of his wife, etc., ending each entry of a too intimate kind with, "Of course, this can't go into the Life." His final entry was to be—"I have decided not to write a Life of Matthew Arnold."

Matthew Arnold then, after Kingsmill had been purged of his fancies by literary agents and publishers, was a comparatively orthodox book. Five years after its publication, in 1933, Arnold's letters to Clough were published, their appearance making it impossible any longer for the most devoted disciple to deny that Arnold had been in love with some girl in Switzerland, had he for some obscure reason wished to do so. The official reaction so far as Kingsmill's biography was concerned was to suggest that he had made an absurd fuss over nothing in particular. But Arnold's love for Marguerite, such as it was, constituted the deepest emotional experience of his life and is therefore of primary importance to any biographer. To assert that the Marguerite episode should have been reduced to triviality is to maintain that a biographer should not be primarily concerned with the individual.

Matthew Arnold is interesting on a further score. In the middle of the book Kingsmill calls "A half-way Halt including A Review of Reviewers." Here he forecasts with fair accuracy some of the various critical reactions to the publication of his biography, and sets out to answer them with the totally unrealistic aim of forestalling all adverse comment on his efforts

—an extraordinary example of how intensely he welcomed sympathetic treatment, and how hypersensitive he was to the type of criticism which, in some passages, he had levelled against Arnold himself. Running like a thread through the book, but most clearly visible in this middle chapter, is the strain of martyrdom which was uppermost on his leaving the family business. Kingsmill appears all the while to be on the defensive and to be going out of his way to antagonize his probable audience so that at the end he could say "There, I told you I was hard done by and misunderstood, and now I've proved it!"

Since his writing both on the poetry of Arnold, and later in his life, on that of many other poets concentrated mainly on unravelling the meaning in their lives, it has been suggested by some critics that he was blind to the patterns of certain word formations or tone-deaf to the rhythms, harmonies and momentum of language. This is quite untrue. It is clearly apparent from his own prose that he was concerned both with verbal style and structural technique as a natural means to his end. But his literary judgment was never beguiled by mere felicity of phrase, by allusive mannerisms or, to use H. W. Fowler's expression, by "elegant variations" into attributing excessive weight of matter to shallow writing prettily presented. Mere terminological dexterity was nothing to him by itself and left him unmoved. The primary object of language, as he saw it, was to convey one's meaning clearly, accurately and with the minimum of fuss, and to underline the meaning with appropriate intonation, resonance and aptitude of idiom. In short, the only valid style was for him the most natural expression of the writer's feelings, his own personal style being distinguished by its economy and its powerful and imaginative use of verbs rather than by any surfeit of ornamental adjectives.

Although the general attitude towards Kingsmill's *Matthew Arnold* has had to undergo some changes with the times, the final verdict has remained substantially the same. One recent biographer of Arnold summed up the academic attitude by stating that Lionel Trilling's study of Arnold is the best which has appeared this century, and Kingsmill's the worst.

Certainly Trilling's *Matthew Arnold* and Kingsmill's are fundamentally different in their biographical approach. Lionel Trilling is an avowed devotee of the encyclopaedic biography so favoured by American scholars and has incorporated similar inflationary tendencies in his own criticism. His study of Arnold he tells us, may be thought of as a biography of Arnold's mind, and whatever purely biographical matter of the more usual type has strayed into the book is incidental to his main intention of clarifying what Arnold really said and meant—though to separate a writer's thought and work from the circumstances of his life may be considered a strange method of finding out what that writer really meant. To fulfil this aim, Professor Trilling subjects Arnold's poetry and prose to a historical and literary criticism by linking them, not exclusively to their author as Kingsmill tried to do, but to the social background against which they were written and to the similar ideas of a number of other writers. The blending of qualities which constitute Arnold's genius is unique not uniform, and two men uttering identical sentences may intend entirely different meanings only to be discerned through a knowledge and understanding of their differing natures. By tracing patterns of thought in the nineteenth century, Professor Trilling gives not so much a biography of Arnold's mind as a chart of his own, for to clarify a man's thought it is not necessary to rephrase his words by a purely intellectual process, but to interpret them with realism and imagination.

The central fallacy of Professor Trilling's study can be seen from his very first chapter. This chapter, based largely on the letters Matthew Arnold wrote to Clough from March 1845 to July 1861, makes the initial point that Arnold in his youth was at the same time deeply melancholic on the one hand and "Jorrockesque" or impishly dandified on the other. What is the nature of this baffling paradox? asks Professor Trilling. Certainly it must be complex. But we must not explore Arnold's nature too closely; far better to raise the paradox above and beyond Arnold the man and examine "the relation of the cockiness to his philosophy."

To unify an essentially divided nature proves a by no means easy operation, and Professor Trilling finds it necessary to push Arnold further and further into the background behind a barrage of literary dialectics. Arnold fades from the pages, the real world is left far distant and the reader finds himself locked in Professor Trilling's literary hothouse.

This method of criticism is of course basically opposed to Kingsmill's who was determined to keep Arnold "chiefly with the help of his poems and letters, continuously before the readers' eyes." In the anxiety he felt to force his unwilling subject to the centre of the stage and hold him there, a kind of scrimmage seems to have developed, with Kingsmill himself clearly visible to the audience, jumping smartly from side to side in his frantic exertions to prevent poor shy Arnold from bolting into one of the side exits. Altogether an untidy and nerve-wracking performance.

Arnold's occasional bursts of gaiety were little more than a half-hearted revolt against the pious and sober training of his father, and his Byronism a mere gesture of filial impiety against the man who could not bring himself to read *Don Juan*. But the depression which took a deeper hold over him as the years advanced sprang from the disharmony produced by the inner and unresolved conflict between his naturally poetic temperament and the puritanical influence of his father's stronger personality. Of the harsh and bitter tone of Arnold's letters to Clough, another indication of this conflict, Professor Trilling makes no mention.

In Kingsmill's view the crux of Arnold's life was reached in his love for Marguerite. His renunciation of her represented the victory of Dr. Arnold's will over his own finer and more sympathetic nature. Professor Trilling's treatment of Marguerite is cursory and disingenuous. After first considering her as merely a literary part of Arnold's poetry, while admitting in parentheses that she was probably a real person, he compares her with Stendhal's Lauriel and Arnold himself with Baudelaire and launches into a series of more such comparisons. After several pages conducted in such style, he gingerly and regretfully approaches Marguerite, the human being. It would be absurd, he says, to maintain that Arnold "did himself an injury" by leaving her, for we possess no data which support the view that she would have made him a presentable or suitable wife. On the other hand, and on another level, Arnold "was giving up an excellent part of himself" in renouncing her. Why and how it is not injurious to give up an excellent part of oneself is not made clear. But in wavering conclusion, Professor Trilling attempts by an extraordinarily unreal compromise to placate all shades of opinion. "Those who believe Marguerite was but a poetical figment and who yet want to give the figment a reality in Arnold's life might consider that she was a symbol of his youthful self."

In a note at this point Professor Trilling refers to Kingsmill's belief that Marguerite was socially inferior to Arnold as "exuberant imagination . . . touched with cheerful malice." Beneath the bantering good-humour of this criticism, there is a dislike which makes itself felt by its petty unfairness. "Mr. Kingsmill," one sentence runs, "is certain that Marguerite was a governess, or a teacher of French, or a paid companion and he bases his certainty upon the belief that Arnold left her because she was of inferior social station." But Kingsmill himself expressed no such "certainty" and the particular paragraph to which Professor Trilling refers is more vague than dogmatic. "She [Marguerite] was, I think, a governess or a companion in a family that was living in Thun; or she may have been a teacher in French, living in apartments. In any case, it is clear that she was not a person of independent means and therefore not a gentlewoman in the strict Victorian sense."

This suggestion of Kingsmill's was based on what Arnold himself had written in his poems. Professor Trilling has also something to say on this aspect. "The evidence of the poems," he writes, "holds good for emotional truth and not for matters of biographic detail." Yet earlier in the chapter he had written, "it is almost impossible to read the poems themselves without being convinced that here is the attempt of a man to tell the truth about an important experience . . . he is a literal poet who tries to say what he means at the moment. . . ." It is another sign of the central flaw to this study that, with both poet and critic straining every nerve for clarity of meaning, literal and emotional, much confusion and uncertainty arises on all questions unconnected with general abstractions.

Where economy and selection are absent, where information replaces insight, writing ceases to be an art and becomes an accumulation. Undeniably Professor Trilling has mapped out some of the backwaters to Arnold's character, but it seems ridiculous to assert that his book is, in the words of W. H. Auden, "the full and final word on Arnold for our generation." Just as his faults spotlight Kingsmill's strength, so his virtues accentuate Kingsmill's shortcomings; Professor Trilling's extraordinary scholarship, his fine intelligence and painstaking efforts throw into sharp relief much that is slipshod and ill-arranged in Kingsmill's biography. But, for the most part, Kingsmill did more harm to himself than to his subject, for having reached any conclusion he straightway announced that it was "obvious", and in the labour of writing it down he grew over-hasty while reporting what he, but not the reader, had already gone through once. So it is that he did not record all the reasons for his conclusions in sufficient detail, and did not follow them up once they were arrived at with fresh evidence which a more prolonged effort would have made available.

Though doubtless partly responsible for this cursory attitude, the urgent need for money which constantly dogged his later life did no more than intensify the natural impatience which lay in Kingsmill's nature and which, even under favourable conditions, would have inclined him to hastiness and trivial inaccuracy.

11

Progress of a Critic

WHILE HE WAS STILL EMPLOYED IN THE FAMILY BUSINESS Kingsmill had planned his own literary career with some considerable thought. He wished to write about six or seven more books in all—one or two novels, a biography of Frank Harris, a book on Wordsworth and a book on Shakespeare, an autobiography, and a long narrative poem, *Reynard and Grimbert.* Of these, he had compiled some sixty-five pages of autobiography, two novels, his *Frank Harris,* a book on Shakespeare (though not in the form he originally intended), and only a few lines of the poem by the time of his death.

He was never able to recommence work on this poem after 1927. Reynard and Grimbert were to be the converse of Don Quixote and Sancho Panza, Grimbert being a little man who felt like a lion. One of the sections he had begun to write was called "Grimbert's Dream," and opened with a picture of Bruges and the chimes.

> "Dispersing wistfully into the night,
> Half echo and half promise of delight."

His aim was to generate enormous lyrical force into this dream as it developed, and to give dramatic humour to it as later told by Grimbert to Reynard.

> "A huge marsh-mallow hit me on the head
> And I was dead, and yet I was not dead.
> It sounds absurd, and yet, indeed, indeed . . .
> No explanations, Grimbert. Pray proceed!
> A huge marsh-mallow hit you on the head,
> And you were dead, and yet you were not dead."

From what little one can see, *Reynard and Grimbert* would have been more successful than the two poems he wrote later in his life. It has greater range and is more succinct. Here is another verse which Kingsmill himself liked very much.

> "But while they drowse in age's fitful sleep,
>   The darkness slowly thins about the keep,
>   Whose steep walls importune the speechless sky,
>   Which pales and crimsons, but does not reply."

Progress on this poem was finally halted shortly before he started his *Matthew Arnold*. In 1928, while still engaged in writing this book, he returned once more to Switzerland, and the following year, while at Thonon-les-Bains, an old market town on the shore of Lake Geneva, he wrote *The Return of William Shakespeare* and *After Puritanism*.

One feels the impossibility of doing proper justice to *The Return of William Shakespeare* without reproducing the book almost as a whole. It is so explicit that any additional commentary seems merely superfluous, and so painstaking, so complete, that fault-finding becomes petty and incongruous. "No one," wrote William Gerhardi in a leading article in *The Bookman,* "who reads . . . *The Return of William Shakespeare* . . . need mourn the past when our own generation yields fruit like Mr. Kingsmill's." Kingsmill's original idea had been to write a play round Shakespeare, and the form which the book eventually took was first suggested by William Gerhardi.

He describes how a scientist has discovered a method of resuscitating the dead, and Shakespeare is brought to life for a period of about six weeks in the year 1943. He never makes any public appearances, but spends the whole of his second lifetime hiding in order to escape from two rival newspaper proprietors who are hoping to exploit him for their own ends. This fantasy of modern publicity includes amusing portraits of Lord Beaverbrook under the name of Lord Westerleigh, and of Lord Rothermere as Lord Youngbrother. In his seclusion

Shakespeare reads what the critics have said about him and delivers a long exposition on the meaning of his works. This contrivance enables Kingsmill to give a full rein to his imaginative powers without causing astonished indignation to his readers as in the case of his *Matthew Arnold*, and incorporates something of the treatment which he originally wanted to apply to Arnold himself. The result is a remarkably well sustained piece of creative literary criticism. Certainly this must rank as one of his very best works, for unlike so much other Shakespearean criticism the conjectures are not purely theoretical or abstract, but true to ordinary life and common sense, and are often marvellously divining. To many of Shakespeare's lines which previously one had overlooked, he adds a new depth of meaning and of beauty.

Kingsmill's aim was to show the relation of Shakespeare's work to his character rather than to give an historical reconstruction of his life or a detailed criticism of each separate play. He was unique among serious Shakespearean commentators in that he constantly attempted to go to the essence of the plays, using numbers of carefully chosen quotations to illustrate the progress of his theme. His criticism adds nothing to Shakespeare that was not already there, neither does it demean nor reduce the poetry by any narrowness of interpretation.

He considered Shakespeare to be at the height of his powers when he wrote *King Lear*, and Kingsmill's account of this play, one of the many enlivening and revealing episodes of the book, perfectly matches his theme. One is tempted to quote whole pages of his powerful and compelling criticism on this and other plays, written as they are in so exact and enriching a prose. The effect of his books and essays, constructed for the most part with elaborate care, is necessarily cumulative rather than piecemeal, so that even the most intelligent choice of quotation must be inadequate in conveying the power and momentum of his prose. But one passage, concise and tailored, must serve here to illustrate something of the directness, humanity and penetration of his critical insight.

"The question which he confronted in *Lear* was the loneliness of man, the final question, to which the family, the nation, and God are the imperfect answers framed by the mass of men as substitutes for their deepest desire, the perfect love of two individuals. . . .

"Lear's sin was the selfishness and vanity in which his desire for love had been entangled. The greater sin of his enemies was that they had ceased to feel their isolation in life, or rather, cherished it, and saw in love a menace to the power based on their isolation.

"The last truth which those who love men learn about their fellow creatures is the first and only truth which the majority of men trouble to master. What his youthful contemporaries in Stratford already knew before he left them, that self-interest is the directing force in most men, is the truth which Shakespeare fully felt when he made Lear break his heart against it. Lear's daughters are the custodians of the social system. Their rejection of him is the rejection of passion by organized self-interest. . . . The conflict between Lear and his daughters is summed up in his cry, 'O ! reason not the need'."

Framed by two sections of pure fiction, the intensity and power of the criticism creates an impelling larger than life impression. It might have been that, by incorporating his Shakespearean criticism in a burlesque novel, Kingsmill hoped to increase his sales, the market for pure literary criticism being what it was and, alas, is. But so far as the critical reception of the book went, comparative silence took the place of abuse. One professor of literature at a Middle Western University, after admitting that he had learnt more about Shakespeare from this work than from almost everything else, went on to express his regret that Kingsmill should have fictionalized his criticism as he had done, an opinion which a number of others shared. But such qualms originate from a very naïve conception of fiction, and possibly a somewhat pompous one of literary criticism.

After writing the first two chapters of *The Return of William Shakespeare,* which introduce Kingsmill himself as Arthur Haigh, the manuscript was temporarily laid aside while he completed his next book, *After Puritanism,* which consists of four long essays over which he took much trouble and time, and which appeared in the same year, 1929, as the Shakespeare book.

The four studies in *After Puritanism* are all informed and penetrating, the theme linking them together—the idea of which had originated during the course of a talk with his friend Arthur Dawe—being Kingsmill's contention that Puritanism "instead of passing tranquilly away round about 1820 was kept alive throughout the Victorian age with artificial stimulants." In his studies of Dean Farrar, Samuel Butler, Frank Harris and W. T. Stead—an oddly assorted quartet if ever there was one—he aimed at illustrating a few of the more important aspects of this contention.

The book opens with a short introduction in which Kingsmill explains in what way each of his chapters supports his view :

> "In *From Shakespeare to Dean Farrar* the points touched upon are the revolt, in Victorian emotionalism over the young, against the Puritan doctrine of general depravity, the growing sense of Christ's humanity, and the rejection of eternal punishment : in *Samuel Butler,* the attack on the Puritan theory of the family, and the questioning of Christian morality as well as Christian theology : in *Frank Harris* the chaos of the late Victorian values, the question of complete verbal licence in literature, and the reappearance of Shakespeare as a human being : in *W. T. Stead,* the attempt of a Puritan born too late to simplify the modern world."

Kingsmill was well qualified to undertake such a work. The first chapter, *From Shakespeare to Dean Farrar,* acts as a form of detailed introduction to the remainder of the book. Although it contains more thought than the other chapters, he was worried lest its relatively subdued tone would affect the readability. His fears were groundless, for the presentation of his material in this opening chapter displays a marked improvement on his *Matthew Arnold*, as will be shown shortly. His favourite chapter was the one dealing with Frank Harris, but that was before his full length study of Harris which, though it does not overlap this earlier essay, considerably outshines it. His aim in *After Puritanism* was not to give a portrait of Harris, but a review of his life together with a criticism of his *The Man Shakespeare*.

In particular his essay on Samuel Butler, though it is apt to deviate in places too far from the avowed theme of the book, is masterly—"this admirably perceptive essay," as Philip Henderson described it in his *Samuel Butler: The Incarnate Bachelor* (1953) "which indicated the main line which any future biographer of Butler must take." While he does not sentimentalize over Butler's temperament which was unfitted to retain or enlarge the celebrity which the publication of *Erewhon* brought him, Kingsmill's sympathy responded to someone who, with all his genius, remained comparatively obscure, who was in revolt against his parents, and whose longing for acclaim culminated only in despair.

Part of the interest in his essay on W. T. Stead is autobiographical, for he and Kingsmill employed similar techniques in endeavouring to achieve opposite results. Stead's mother seems to have been in some ways similar to Kingsmill's, one of her friends summing her up in words which could apply equally to Lady Lunn : "A life very simple, very placid in its deeds of week-day holiness, yet most powerful in its shaping influence upon the fiery, ardent nature of her son." Stead, like Kingsmill, never wrote and seldom spoke about his mother, but whereas Stead made it his practice to publish at regular intervals some fresh tribute to his father's virtues, Kingsmill was in the habit of composing parental reprimands inadequately concealed under the guise of generalization, and of giving out open verbal caricatures of Sir Henry Lunn.

As an example of this first habit, the following sentence which occurs near the beginning of the essay on Stead will suffice : "In an epoch," Kingsmill wrote, "of varied achievements, scientific, literary, and commercial, the elect of God related themselves to mundane reality almost exclusively through their aptitude for money-making; balancing their imperfect contact with a complex epoch by self-complacency."

To illustrate Kingsmill's use of humour which inflated his father's personality up to the dimensions of a buffoon, one need only quote the story he told to Hesketh Pearson in 1941, when they went to Harrow while working on their talk and travel book, *This Blessed Plot*. As they were walking towards the hill by a narrow passage, Kingsmill remarked, "I don't expect you to dance with excitement over what I am about to tell you, but this is the way my father used to go to and from the railway station every morning for twenty years or so. Sir Frederick Kenyon, who was the keeper of the manuscripts in the British Museum, used to cover the same ground with him. Keeping manuscripts probably does not go with a strong desire for small talk just after breakfast. At any rate, my father used frequently to complain that Kenyon walked too fast for him. He did not put the suspicion into words, but there was something in the tone of his complaint which suggested a doubt whether Kenyon was naturally a fast walker." W. T. Stead, together with Frank Harris and Boswell, he considered as the most outstanding oddities in history, describing his father as "a second-class oddity," and adding, "I hope that's not mere filial piety."

Stead's hyperboles in memory of his father annoyed Kingsmill as Matthew Arnold's praise of Dr. Arnold had done earlier. "The imaginative basis of Puritanism," he wrote, "is the relation of the Father, God, and the Son, Christ. . . . Puritanism smugness derived naturally from the self-approval proper to the elect of God. . . . In exhibiting his father and his son to the public as perfect human beings . . . Stead illustrates . . . this self-complacency." But even with the satirical image of Sir Henry Lunn firmly fixed before his eyes, Kingsmill himself does not always escape from his own brand of smugness. After the publication of *Matthew Arnold* his father tried to discourage him from writing. "You'll never make a living writing books," he said, "now I made £1,000 in my first year at journalism."

"That's why I am writing books," Kingsmill answered.

The difference of presentation and essentially of the state of mind in which *Matthew Arnold* and *After Puritanism* were written is very great. The author of *Matthew Arnold* was on the defensive against an unappreciative and hostile atmosphere created by those of his family who had consistently undervalued him in the past, and also against the anticipated rebuffs of the critics which, he seems at times to have realized, his defensive attitude would inevitably call forth. The self-consciousness of the writing was increased by the lack of necessary reference books and personal information to be found in Thonon. *After Puritanism*, on the other hand, was completed in comparative tranquillity. The raw material for his book was, to a large extent, his own past years, and the encouragement he needed was forthcoming from his friend Arthur Dawe.

The academicians to whom *Matthew Arnold* had been sent found themselves reading in the very first chapter—*Sanctity of Private Life under Queen Victoria*—that "in calling a prostitute an 'unfortunate' the Victorians wished to imply that a prostitute was someone who had invested in the wrong stock, in spite of the advice of more experienced investors." In the previous paragraph, too, they had been told how "Dickens's 'unfortunates' emerge suddenly out of the night to gaze with hungry despair at the face of a Rose Maylie or a Little Dorrit . . . then back into the pitchy blackness with a wild unearthly cry; leaving the modern reader to wonder at the nerves of tempered steel the Victorian roué must have possessed to get into bed against odds like these."

Having continued in this vein for some pages, Kingsmill ends the chapter by explaining that he has not pictured the actual world of the Victorians but their ideal world. "These things did not occur, but it gratified the Victorians to believe they did. In such an atmosphere Casanova himself would have become reticent, and Benvenuto Cellini vague."

In *After Puritanism* he had altered these opinions very little. The writing is as entertaining as ever, but his conclusions are backed up by evidence, the tone is less uneven and while it does not lose in wit it gains in interest. Before leading the reader through the detailed findings of a certain heroic clergyman, the Reverend G. P. Merrick, who took upon himself the task of interviewing some sixteen thousand and twenty-two prostitutes, Kingsmill sums up his own view of the Victorian attitude:

"The theory that prostitutes were the victims of male lust was an unavoidable corollary of the convention that women of gentle birth were free from original sin. The same freedom had, logically, to be conceded to women of the lower orders, with male depravity, and especially aristocratic male depravity, to account for the numerous exceptions that seem to contradict this theory. A prostitute was 'unfortunate' in the same sense that someone stunned by a falling tile, or knocked over by a runaway horse, was unfortunate.

"This attitude has not even the advantage of alleviating the unhappiness of a prostitute's life. To the girl it was oppressive to feel that a sinful woman was a *lusus naturae;* and the man, submitting to the power of suggestion, was apt to behave more brutally than he would have behaved in a natural atmosphere."

In this passage the real and the ideal Victorian world are brought into line and presented in just proportion. In *The Sanctity of Private Life under Queen Victoria* the ideal world is offered up as a sacrifice to Kingsmill's powers of satire and his exuberant wit.

After the failure of *Matthew Arnold*, he was unable to find a publisher in America for *After Puritanism*, the market for what they called "quick-fire biographies" being almost negligible. "Apparently original information goes best with publishers," he commented ruefully, "until one is established. A packet of unpublished letters dealing with the views on manure formed by Samuel Butler in New Zealand would have helped."

12

The Anthologist

IN ADDITION TO THESE TWO BOOKS OF BIOGRAPHY AND LITERARY criticism, Kingsmill brought out the first of his amusing and original anthologies, *Invective and Abuse* the same year. Ironically enough this book, being a collection of other people's expressions of anger ranging from John Skelton to Geoffrey Howard, was alone of all his others a comparative success, Sir Oswald Mosley, it is said, becoming enthusiastic over it to the extent of forwarding a copy to Hitler. Another instalment, *More Invective*, followed the next year and a combined version was published as late as 1944. Hesketh Pearson, writing on the Kingsmill anthologies in a foreword to *The High Hill of the Muses*, says that "Kingsmill himself became a little restless when people praised his volume of vituperation," and Kingsmill, in a short preface to the last edition of *Invective and Abuse*, tells us that he often used to meet people who said that of course they knew his work—"that thing of yours on abuse."

None of his subsequent anthologies achieved the same degree of success as this first one. Due to his wide reading and retentive memory, he was able to complete many of these anthologies extremely quickly, in sharp contrast to his other books which, for the most part, were slowly and laboriously put together. So pressing at times were his financial commitments that some of these anthologies were finished in a matter of three or four weeks. When Hesketh Pearson wished to look at a proof of his *Parents and Children*, Kingsmill replied, "I have not yet seen the anthology, and shall look at it with interest, for I have only the faintest idea of what it is about, to say nothing of its contents. That is one advantage of working under pressure. I imagine that Balzac and Scott were frequently to be observed reading their respective works with eyes starting out of their heads with excitement."

What they said at the time, with its page long preface and few short editorial comments can have taken little longer than *Parents and Children* to compile, but *Courage* and *Made on Earth*, his anthology on marriage, are more fully and carefully annotated and both contain interesting introductions. Most amusing of all his anthologies though is *The Worst of Love* which consists of numerous specimens of insincere writing in poetry and prose on the subject of love. "Little would be left of this volume," he wrote, "were one to remove the contributions of those inflexible spirits who say what they do not feel, and feel what they do not say." Kingsmill's sharp eye for hypocrisy and cant is responsible for an entertaining introduction and many witty and appreciative notes throughout the book which add greatly to the fun. Illustrated by Nicolas Bentley, *The Worst of Love* stands favourable comparison in its chosen field with D. B. Wyndham Lewis's and Charles Lee's better known anthology, *The Stuffed Owl*, which came out the previous year and which it resembles in some respects.

"A critic if the highest order is provided with an Ithuriel spear which discriminates the sham sentiments from the true," wrote Leslie Stephen in an essay on Pope. It was such a quality, clearly apparent even in this anthology, which singled Kingsmill out from the ranks of literary politicians of his day, who, like women searching after the right clothes for a particular season or occasion, were primarily concerned with making or breaking the various short-lived literary fashions. Their criticism may become part of literary history; Kingsmill's is a valuable contribution to literature itself. "But criticism of this kind," Leslie Stephen adds, "as Pope truly says, is as rare as poetical genius." For, by virtue of their deep and rapid intuitional response to the truth, the two are closely allied.

Contemporary reputation and success are achieved as much by superficial traits as by genuine attainments. Kingsmill's criticism does not startle one with exaggerated headlines. He believed that an author's work could best be judged by relating it to its source with which he partially identified his own state, and not to its effect distorted by the prevailing political and social conditions of the present. The standards by which he took his judgment were at the same time more personal and less ephemeral, but in a collectivist age their value was never recognized. What might be termed in modern day jargon as "an uncommitted writer", the intricate blending of humour and melancholy, sensitivity and austerity, mysticism and shrewdness which distinguished his work was too complex and individual to be satisfactorily classified into any known type. Moreover he fought in no Spanish war, joined no pacifist or intellectual gatherings at Garsington and Gower Street, never inhabited Bloomsbury. Critics were unable or unwilling to believe that he was not a member of any literary faction, a Left or Right Book Club say, or, being eventually persuaded that this was the case, refused to consider him seriously. And in their quick muddled way they put him down simultaneously as an imitator of Lytton Strachey and an amateur Freudian. But if posterity, with its ebb and flow, is the final arbiter of man's achievements, then the impoverished neglect of Hugh Kingsmill will be placed high in the annals of literary destitution.

But that this state of affairs was due to his shortcomings as well as his virtues seems probable, for the position of isolation brought about by his courage in remaining consistently guided by his own powers of imagination was strengthened by his will to succeed. It was his ambition which made him occasionally adopt too dominant a tone, which drove him sometimes to be over-assertive and inflexible and which hindered him from reviewing his contemporary novelists. And as he ignored them, so the eminent figures of the literary world overlooked him. With a majority of the leading critics of his day he had no dealings whatever. George Orwell he met only at the end of their lives; on the single occasion he met Wyndham Lewis, then in the trough of persecution mania, he was suspected of poison-

ing the food; and he described his three encounters with T. S.
Eliot as similar to audiences given by the Pope to some obscure
member of a Nonconformist Church on a visit to Rome.

Possibly the most valuable of all his anthologies are the
posthumously published *The High Hill of the Muses* for its long
and stimulating introduction on English literature together
with its interesting selection of Kingsmill's "favourite passages
from English literature which have survived corroding or puri-
fying effects of time," and his *Johnson without Boswell*. The
aim of this latter work was to present a picture of Johnson
from several contemporary sources outside Boswell—Sir John
Hawkins, Mrs. Thrale, Anna Seward, Arthur Murphy, Sir
Joshua Reynolds, Fanny Burney and others, including extracts
from Johnson's own prayers and meditations, his letters and
childhood reminiscences. This book uncovers a greater depth of
humanity and sympathy in Johnson's nature than is ever discernible in Boswell's *Johnson*. The intention was in no way to
disparage Boswell for whose qualities he held a great admiration, but to qualify the unstinted praise given to Boswell's *Life
of Johnson* by such highly esteemed writers as Macaulay and
Carlyle. Boswell's insistence on Johnson's verbal ascendancy
tended to further the impression that he was the bigoted cham-
pion of social conventions and the established order, and to
obscure his individuality; for to Boswell he was always more of
a character than a man. Moreover Boswell had been unfair
to at least two of his rival biographers, Mrs. Thrale and Sir
John Hawkins. Boswell's *Life* is less a biography than a journal,
and Kingsmill intended to follow up this volume with another,
Johnson with Boswell which, as Hesketh Pearson writes, "would
have shown Boswell's real merit by omitting all the non-Bos-
wellian material from the *Life* and the *Tour of the Hebrides*."

The only remaining anthology which Kingsmill edited, *The
English Genius*, is comprised of some fourteen essays on a
variety of topics, all written specifically for this particular collection. A symposium of this nature had not been his original
plan, but as often happened his first ideas were modified and

adapted to come more in line with the publisher's requirements. Several years before the book was published, it had
occurred to him that it should be possible to bring out an
English Bible which, by containing extracts from English
poets, musicians, historians, lawyers, scientists and so on, would
provide an expression of the English national character com-
parable to that contained in the Hebrew Bible. The original
title, *The English Bible*, was soon discarded on the grounds
that, in the first place, it carried with it the suggestion of boredom and, in the second, a large majority of the English already
referred to the Hebrew Bible as the English Bible, and though
vaguely aware that it was, in point of fact, a Hebrew production, seldom cared to be reminded of it. An ambiguous association with *Burke's Peerage* was also feared. Nevertheless Kingsmill was stubbornly convinced that his idea would command
a wide appeal. He saw the book as cheaply priced, studded
with brilliant passages culled from the most distinguished
authors and celebrated personages, decked with a fine array
of lavish illustrations, greeted everywhere with long congratulatory eulogies and selling briskly on all bookstalls.

The English Genius which appeared in 1939 embodied an
idea substituted in place of the original one. It contained essays
on such subjects as Climate and Character, Painting, Monarchy
and War by a number of well-known authors including Hilaire
Belloc (Verse), Rose Macaulay (Moral Indignation), W. R.
Inge (Religion) and Rebecca West (Snobbery), and "it may be
regarded," Kingsmill wrote, "as an introduction to my original
idea, and a stimulus for someone to put it into execution." Two
subjects which are unfortunately omitted from the collection
are music and architecture. Kingsmill had wanted Ernest New-
man for the first and John Betjeman for the second, while he
himself proposed to write on poetry. But when the anthology
finally appeared, he contributed only a general introduction.

Apart from these published anthologies he was engaged at
the time of his death in producing yet another one, *The Genius
of Carlyle*, "the keeper of the Victorian conscience," as he called

him, "a strange conscience and a strange keeper." Kingsmill
never read Carlyle when young and had hardly looked at him
before his late thirties. But in the early nineteen thirties he read
David Wilson's monumental life of Carlyle which interested
him considerably and encouraged him to start reading Carlyle
seriously and thoroughly for the first time. What appealed to
him immediately was Carlyle's courageous ability to shock
conventional views both with his forthright actions and his
strong opinions expressed with that "half poetic, half-humour-
ous fascination." But as time went by and he reached a deeper
understanding of the man he came to perceive, to use Hesketh
Pearson's phrase, "every turn and twist in Carlyle's character,
especially his semi-conscious humour." In fact Carlyle's complex nature fascinated Kingsmill. "Inextricably involved with
the dour opportunist," he wrote of him in his introduction to
The High Hill of the Muses, "whose inherited Calvinism made
him condemn the world and whose innate conceit made him
despise its inhabitants was a keen-eyed poet who found the
universal not in windy generalities but in particular details, and
a humorist absorbed in the idiosyncrasies of individuals." So it
is reasonable to assume that *The Genius of Carlyle* would have
consisted predominantly of material selected from Carlyle's
journals and letters rather than from his formal works where
the "dyspeptic prophet" and not the poet and humorist was in
command.

The chief interest for Kingsmill himself in these anthologies
centred round the advance he received for them. He would
swiftly foist one of them on the unfortunate publisher who was
printing his most recent book, or, failing this, select some
peculiarly obscure and unsuspecting one to favour with his
attentions. Under this continual pressure his spirit seldom
flagged until, perhaps, the very end of his life. William Ger-
hardie, in his *Resurrection* published in 1935, wrote :

"Kingsmill's society was worth to me that of all my
other friends put together. There was a steady glow about

this man which illuminated all life around him, so that
in his presence you walked as if in a little circle of light
independent of the hour or the seasons; and indeed he
himself seemed perpetually cheered by this light emanating
from him, so that he had to ask himself, with a sigh, how
it was that in the midst of his financial predicaments he
was beaming with joy."

But to pretend that these increasing financial predicaments
following so abruptly upon a life of comparative prosperity
had no effect on him would be stupid and unrealistic. Both his
life and his writing was affected by the change, as two examples
will show. Shortly before the Second World War, on the death
of Sir Henry Lunn, Arnold Lunn gave Kingsmill their late
father's gold watch, though he himself as the elder brother was
legally entitled to it. Sir Henry Lunn's estate was negligible,
and Kingsmill promptly accepted the watch as a gift, then later
sold it back to his brother, after a dispute over the price, for
£25. Moreover, whenever he borrowed money from other
people, as he quite frequently did, he was inclined to consider
any repayment of the sum he had been lent as an entirely
separate transaction requiring something to be handed over to
him in exchange. Friends, relations and publishers were *in loco
parentis* so far as finance was concerned. He expected to get
from publishers in particular what his father was unwilling
or unable to give him. And, from his point of view, he managed
them very ably. From Jonathan Cape, Robert Hale and Macdonald he certainly received advances without supplying any
books, and from Methuen's alone he received a number of such
sums. "Annually when our auditors checked our books," wrote
Alan White of Methuen's, "I was asked by my boss to account
for these sums. Piqued by his tone, I said tartly that works of
the imagination could not be written with mechanical regu-
larity. He stared for a full minute at his papers, and then
remarked, without the trace of a smile (though he was not
without humour on subjects unconnected with business):

'Works of the imagination is right'." And when, eventually, a book was produced, it was written so well and it sold so badly that the publisher was reduced to despair. He was, in the words of Rupert Hart-Davis, "the publisher's nightmare."

Although Kingsmill inherited a certain business flair from his father, which he most successfully employed in extracting advances from various publishers for somewhat improbable books, he never managed to free himself from a state of pecuniary embarrassment during his life, and remained unable to write many of the books that he would have wished. At least part of the difficulty lay in the bad feeling which his irresponsible dealings with several publishers promoted. The late Mr. Jonathan Cape told the present author that in his opinion Kingsmill was neither a very pleasant personality nor a writer of any great talent, but on further questioning admitted never having known him or read his books. Rather naïvely perhaps I pressed him to explain his views, at which he pointed out that Kingsmill had never fully completed the autobiography for which he had been given an advance by his firm; and he handed me the original contract with the air of a magistrate producing a criminal document. Choosing to belittle the several years between the signing of this contract and Kingsmill's illness and death, I cried, "But he died!" He looked at me coldly for what seemed a very long time. "And whose fault was that?" he finally demanded.

Kingsmill's unending money difficulties were also aggravated to some extent by the fact that he always appeared to live on a scale which one would not normally associate with the profession of a struggling literary critic, his various flats and homes in some of the following years seeming often spacious and comfortable if not actually luxurious. His constant lack of any great amount of money affected him not so much materialistically, but mentally in his wondering anticipation of how he and his family were to continue living as they had done in the past. What he was compelled for the rest of his life to endure is perhaps best suggested by Hilaire Belloc's definition of poverty:

"It is a state of mind in which a man is perpetually anxious for the future of himself and his dependents, unable to pursue life upon a standard to which he was brought up, tempted both to subservience and sour revolt, and tending inexorably towards despair."

13

The Fool of Love

THOSE WHO DISBELIEVE IN THE PRACTICAL ADVANTAGES OF
the married state over bachelorhood, or who query its suit-
ability to men and women of outstanding ability, might well
instance Kingsmill's uneasy life as an obvious and conclusive
confirmation of their opinion. His own attitude to this question
was far from consistent; when detached his most general and
charitable verdict on marriage seeming to have been that while
it was a difficult and even unnatural arrangement, yet it was
the best practical compromise available on this earth and that
therefore one should adapt oneself to its demands as best one
could. There was enough truth, he felt, to disturb the thoughtful bachelor in Johnson's view that unmarried men, as the out-
laws of human society, were certain to be miserable, but not
certain to be devout. He avowed, too, the wisdom of Johnson's saying that "marriage is the best state for a man in
general, and every man is a worse man in proportion as he is
unfit for the married state." Judged by such a standard Kingsmill does not emerge any too triumphantly, for while he loved
his home as a headquarters in which to rest between romantic
sallies he could never resign himself to the daily requirements
of the married state, the regular nagging routine of which pal-
led on him after a time, and though he could not live without
a woman, he found it extremely difficult to live with one. He
was intensely aware of the limiting, incarcerable and even
stifling nature of marriage all his adult life. While a prisoner
of war he wrote :

". . . society fears love for the same reason as the young
worship it. Love to it is like a fire—safe in the grate,

125

ruinous everywhere else; and when the fire of love is confined in the grate of marriage, the individual may do with
it what he likes, burn it wastefully, choke it so that it
smoulders without light or warmth, let it die to ashes.
That does not concern society, society being contented as
long as the house is not set on fire to the prejudice of the
general safety."

Thus, while the institution of marriage appealed to his objective reasoning as a workable compromise, it appeared to his
emotionalism to be an obstacle to "the key of unrestricted
freedom, infinite lawless enjoyment, roaming the wide earth
in search of satisfaction."

Part of this restlessness sprang from his rose-coloured, idealistic view of women. Like Cervantes, he was idealistic in his
conduct and realistic only in retrospect. Even when speaking
of some girl of whom he was fond, his voice would take on a
soft and tender note as if he was referring to a child, and his
overwhelming susceptibility to the charms of attractive women
in general betrayed the precarious emotional nature of a temperament similar in some degree to that of Hazlitt and illustrated at the same time both what was weakest and best in his
character. As for his love-letters, he once remarked in a
moment of detachment that "for sentiment they would make
Barrie blush, and for imbecility they would make the inmates
of Colney Hatch sit up and take notice."

Kingsmill was, on the whole, attractive himself to women.
True, he could not at one stroke unite the appeal of romanticism with the advantages of practical security, but a writer
is always something of a romantic figure, and Kingsmill's
powers of optimistic eloquence were certainly reassuring. Besides which, he always noticed what a woman was wearing,
remarked on how lovely she looked, seemed to respect her as
a human being—her mind even—and by such measures generally masked his gullibility.

Kingsmill's character was curious; he was a sensualist and

a humanist but he combined the sensibility and fine intelligence of the introvert with the breezy vitality of the extrovert. At the same time, while he steadfastly believed that he was continually being cheated out of real love, always narrowly missing the only worthwhile goal in life, there must be many who would give a lot to possess a temperament which could command at will similar opportunities for disappointment. The disharmony in Kingsmill's nature crystallized in his permanent sense of loss, and was rooted in the division which existed between his immature emotions and fully developed intellect. It is one thing to believe that in love and love alone lies the salvation of man; it is quite another to snatch with eager impulsiveness on both sides at the gifts which nature has set to the right hand and to the left. Only when his intellect was in the ascendant, supported and not overwhelmed by his feelings, could he become detached enough to see marriage in a charitable light. But had he possessed fewer faults he might have made an excellent husband, and a second-rate writer.

In 1930 Kingsmill married Miss Dorothy Vernon by whom he was to have two daughters and a son. His second wife, a very different woman from his first, had met him as the result of her admiration for his short novels in *The Dawn's Delay*, a year or two before. With her he settled down first in a small house, *"Les Sapins"*, "not inelegantly situated and with all mediaeval conveniences," and then, following an altercation with their landlord, in a pretty pink villa called *"Rien et Tout,"* on the tableland of Thonon, some two hundred feet above Lake Geneva and commanding a view in all directions. Here they remained for the next two and a half years, living on only a few shillings a day.

Keenly interested in literature, the second Mrs. Kingsmill had, before meeting her husband, completed a novel herself, the manuscript of which she handed to him and which he shortly afterwards mislaid on a tube train. It was a good example of the devastating vagueness and still-unconceded practical incompetence of his behaviour which, even if it did

not disconcert his wife too much initially, must at times have
tried sorely the patience of any woman. Kingsmill was a sensitive and an honourable man; but he was also tactless, and his
persistent and elementary disregard for the least attractive
aspects of the "empirical world" often extended beyond the
bounds of reason. The workings of his conscience, too, were
subtle and idiosyncratic. The lyical, melancholy, yet invin-
cibly optimistic sense of longing that persuaded him to place
a long way first on the list of urgent priorities his own personal
happiness (except where it seemed possible to place it coinci-
dent and on a par with that of some newly-encountered beautiful girl) was based on an uncertain instinct, distorted and led
astray by his oppressive, sanctimonious upbringing. Nor, in the
face of censure, did he trouble to exonerate himself, identifying
any particular failing of which he might reasonably stand
accused with a natural pervading malady universal to man,
and with which he, as a man, was naturally imbued. Happiness,
both within and beyond the confines of matrimony, was, he
believed, contagious. It could not be forced upon mankind in
arbitary didactic fashion, nor spread socialogically over everyone in a thin impersonal stream. Of the two selfish choices
allowed one, egocentricity was always preferable to egotism, in
any of its philanthropic guises. The best way to promote happiness was therefore to be happy oneself; and if he failed in some
degree by these oblique methods to render everyone content,
then it was less a shortcoming of his romantic philsophy than
of his *locus*: "My heart's in the right place. But I am not."

His elusiveness as a husband—a constant manœuvring, as it
were, into "the right place"— was another sign of this enslave-
ment to the illusions of his early years. His love, too, of par-
titioning off his life into several water-tight compartments,
while unfortunate in the mistrustful atmosphere it produced
between his friends and his family, was possibly also open to
misinterpretation. To a large extent he was a conventional
man, highly susceptible to the comforts and amenities of marriage. But the family did not satisfy his whole nature, and he

felt tormented at times by the rather abstract notion that it was acting as some sort of unnatural handicap to his fuller, more complete enjoyment of things. This ambivalent and logically inconsistent attitude could occasionally startle and perplex even those who thought they knew him most intimately.

The fact that his wife interested herself in literary matters, coupled with his own very natural wish to be found in agreement with her, may have increased his unwillingness to appear in her company and that of a number of his friends simultaneously. The tight-rope of diplomacy on which he felt himself obliged to balance under such circumstances seemed too incongruous and painful to him. Though Kingsmill did most of his actual writing at the Authors' Club in Whitehall Court—which was swelled over the years by members who joined chiefly to enjoy his company—it would be wrong to imagine that he did not value domestic comforts or that he preferred other surroundings to those of his own home. Domesticity appealed to him strongly and intermittently, whenever his sense of what he wished life to be was obliterated by his sense of what it was. The most reasonable explanation for a marital state of affairs which is by no means uncommon is suggested by Byron :

"Man's love is of man's life a thing apart,
'Tis woman's whole existence."

The difficulties and complexities of Kingsmill's temperament were aggravated by the constant corroding anxiety of how to combine a career in literature with the maintenance of himself, his wife and eventually a family of two sons and two daughters. Though he was able to earn more money on his return to England, the cost of living was of course correspondingly higher. While foundering under the attrition of cumulative petty worries, increasing attentions were being paid to him on his door step by duns and importuning tradesmen in inverse proportion to the neglect accorded him by critics and readers. It was a wearing existence, though he was fortified, he once remarked, by the good example of Fielding, who rarely ventured into the street on weekdays, Sunday being a red-letter day on which duns were legally prohibited from serving writs. To alleviate their poverty, Dorothy Kingsmill opened up a dressmaking business, but the profits appear to have been unspectacular and it was in any case put an end to by the war. His friends, also, did what they could to help. Malcolm Muggeridge offered to mortgage his own house in order to lend him money; Hesketh Pearson vainly put him up for the vacant librarianship at the House of Lords; William Gerhardi persuaded Lord Beaverbrook to employ him as book critic on the *Sunday Express*—but not for long. "He [Beaverbrook] has what I want, but does he want what I have?" queried Kingsmill wryly. At other times he would come along with some enthusiastic and improbable scheme of his own—an unspecified collaboration with H. G. Wells, for instance, commissioned on the strength of Wells's substantial reputation and with a fittingly substantial advance on royalties to be divided equally between the co-authors on signature of the contract.

The tribulations of penury, the disappointments of literary neglect, the agitations of his undimmed romantic longings were concealed however beneath a misleadingly bluff exterior. Though he was naïvely unaware of how to employ to his own practical and economic advantage his gifts of sympathy, his sense of life and knowledge of character, he was loved by all those who knew him intimately—loved not just sentimentally despite or because of his faults and eccentricities, but as a man of many subtle facets to his personality, a man who illumined life with fresh interest, animation and humour. "Hughie had a prodigious gift for fantasy," John Davenport records—"what Italians call 'improvising'. These free and often Rabelaisian rhapsodies were very revealing. For example, he would invent some ludicrous incident in the sexual life of the Carlyles, say, or the Brownings. His audience would be speechless with laughter as the imagery built up into a grotesque climax, and H.K. himself might have tears pouring down his pink cheeks; then he would pause, and utter his mournful, tender, immensely understanding : 'Poor old man!' This invariably provoked a sympathetic silence. Followed, of course, by increased, and even more helpless, laughter from us all. This mixture of understanding, a blend of affectionate insight and a refusal to be hoodwinked, together with his sense of the absurdities of the human condition seemed to me, as a young man, uniquely his own."

It was at such moments of imaginative fantasy that, lifted above the meaner sordid actualities of his career, he could see life steadily and see it whole. And then, all the confusing and troubled ambitions of the will appeared to him as a mere gratification of lust and power; while the pursuits of the soaring imagination were the attainment of love and truth. The will, with its passion to dominate and possess, left only chaos and division. But through the imagination, which yearned for union with another life, he believed that we might apprehend a harmony which envelops and gives meaning to our present worldly existence.

14

Biography and Parody

WHILE AT THONON KINGSMILL WROTE HIS WAR MEMOIRS, *Behind Both Lines, Frank Harris*, and a number of parodies, articles and book reviews for various English and American periodicals.

Behind Both Lines is entertaining and light-hearted. The diverting candour which runs through it was refreshing after so many years of the more formal accounts of war experiences, drenched in rodomontade about military glory. "I asked Major Asquith whether he wished me to lead the company or to direct operations from the rear," one passage ran. "He selected the second alternative; I am glad that, for once, my private inclinations coincided with my military duties." On the other hand, he did not exaggerate unnecessarily the military absurdities which surrounded him or his own incompetence as a soldier. His quietly humorous attitude throughout the book can be seen very well from his account of the first parade in France taken by a new C.O. shortly after he himself had become acting Company commander.

"As acting Company commander, I was provided, against my will and better judgment, with a horse. Sterndale Bennett had returned to England for a few weeks, and our new C.O. was a cavalry colonel. My horse, fortunately a very phlegmatic animal, had this disadvantage, that when he resolved to be recalcitrant he was far too insensitive to bother about my hauling on his bit. There was a violent downpour at the first parade presided over by the new C.O. The rain drove slantingly into our eyes as we faced the colonel and after a moment's reflection my horse began to pivot slowly round. I struggled to keep him head on, but uselessly, and he ceased to rotate only when he and I were facing my company. The colonel did not refer to this obscene incident."

The biography of Frank Harris, his once venerated master, is most skilfully written and put together. The idea of writing Harris's life had occupied his mind on and off for nearly fifteen years before the book was finally completed. As early as 1923 he was musing on it "daily in my bath," and by the following year he had worked out a format. The delay in writing it was occasioned less by the fact that Harris was still alive than by his anxiety to create a really good and lasting work of literature. He saw in Harris the subject of a classic biography second only to Boswell's Johnson. Harris was a superb failure, a man of prodigious energy and vitality and a compendium of every form of charlatanism rampant in the complicated civilization of 1880 to 1914. "To picture him," he said, "will be to picture one of the most interesting ages in history. He is the colour-blind chameleon of the age, and I shall record the lines of the carpet, and the hues, ill-matching, which the ambitious but myopic Frankie assumed, leaping from patch to patch."

Although some space is devoted to Harris's non-fiction, there is little enough dealing with his novels and short stories, of which Kingsmill did not think very highly. "I want to pick what is really good in the old boy's work and character," he told Hesketh Pearson who had also been a disciple of Harris, "perhaps I might devote an appendix, two pages in large print, to this part of my subject."

The book, when it did appear, was brilliantly written. Each word of every sentence is carefully chosen and subtly placed so as to achieve a mingling of accuracy, wit and humour. The humour indeed is sympathetic throughout, seeming, as Kingsmill himself wrote of Chaucer's "at the same time to reveal and excuse the weakness of men."

Much of the spirit in which Kingsmill set about writing Harris's life comes out in the remark he made on the news that

Harris was dying. "One feels," he said, "that the old boy has had a good run for everybody else's money, and that old age is depressing him, and he'll be better in his last and for the first time otherwise untenanted bed." In the late spring of 1927, during his wanderings through France, Kingsmill had met Harris in Nice for the last time. There is much tenderness as well as humour in his account of this meeting where Harris, aged seventy-two, spoke to him at length though without all his old animation and on less exalted topics than when they had last talked in the days of *Hearth and Home*.

At first Harris had not recognized Kingsmill, and as he was approached his expression, Kingsmill noted, became tense, "as of a man prepared to be arrested on almost any charge." As he drew nearer still, the car in which Harris and his wife were sitting began to move. Kingsmill held up his hand with considerable authority and the car jerked uneasily to a halt. Feeling by now perfectly calm he thrust his head boldly through the window and a conversation developed between the three of them, Harris maintaining that he should return at five o'clock, Mrs. Harris repeating that neither of them would be back by five o'clock and Kingsmill adding now and again that whereas five o'clock would be admirable as far as he himself was concerned, he had no wish to cause excessive inconvenience and could doubtless manage to call the following day. Eventually it was agreed by a majority of two to one that he could return at five o'clock for tea. The car started to move off but again stopped when a sudden bellow issued from Harris, who, it transpired, had failed to recognize him during their conversation, a failure which he attributed partly to Kingsmill having aged and put on flesh, and partly to his own failing memory, Kingsmill himself inclining to the latter hypothesis. Mrs. Harris at this point took advantage of the extra time to voice once more her unshaken conviction that she and her husband would not have returned by five o'clock, but this slogan had become too threadbare by now and no one took any notice of her.

At five o'clock punctually Kingsmill returned to the Villa to find Harris and his wife having tea with an admirer from Lancashire, a man of about fifty named Hooton who had apparently travelled to Nice for no other reason than meeting Harris. Harris himself was sitting in an armchair when he entered, his legs covered with numerous rugs. While Kingsmill seated himself and was pouring out some tea, Mrs. Harris having briefly indicated the teapot as she hurried from the room, Harris commenced to deliver himself on the subject of phlebitis. Soon the topic changed and he spoke in turn of Bottomley, Churchill, Alfred Douglas, Arnold Bennett and H. G. Wells. Kingsmill meanwhile was discovering that his own taste for monologue had diminished, and insisted on some share of the conversation. Hooton, too, sitting to one side with the four volumes of Harris's *My Life and Loves* suitably autographed for him close at hand, ventured occasionally to interpolate some trifling remark.

"I was glad to see the old ruffian again," Kingsmill records. When he got up to leave Harris rose too from his couch and drawing him to one side out of earshot from the still sedentary Lancastrian, asked him if he had liked the third and fourth volumes of his autobiography as well as the second. "I said I preferred the second," Kingsmill wrote, "lowering my voice so that the new disciple might not overhear the blasphemous suggestion that the master was not always on the heights. Harris nodded, looking like a conspiratorial urchin. My heart warmed to him as we shook hands for what I felt was the last time."

The closing paragraphs of Kingsmill's book reveal, too, the underlying affection which he held for his subject, for affection always shows through his writing where there is little to envy. Harris's fate, like Johnson's, was little to be desired on the whole, and Kingsmill's sympathy was free to expand. Only occasionally does he deliberately score off Harris, for this type of writing necessitated an over-simplification of character which would dilute the humour and was therefore not to his own advantage. He found much in Harris that was, if not admir-

able, at least endearing, and, at the end of this biography his
tone is mellow and gentle :

"It was summer as Harris drew to the end of his task
[his life of Bernard Shaw] and sometimes, he says, he
would dodge the weary grind to sit in the sun outside a
café. The passing girls and the blue sea might stir memories
of former days, but life was fast slipping away, with all
he had felt in it, and all he had tried to feel, lust and
power, Shakespeare and Jesus. Or if any saying of Jesus
still remained in his mind it was one which had not previously concerned him : 'Verily, verily, I say unto thee,
when thou wast young, thou girdest thyself, and walkest
wither thou wouldest : but when thou shalt be old, thou
shalt stretch forth thy hands, and another shall gird thee,
and carry thee whither thou wouldest not.'

"On the last afternoon of his life, round about five
o'clock, he roused himself from the coma into which he
had collapsed, and snatching up a glass flung it against
the wall. Hearing the crash, his wife hurried in and found
him leaning back against the bed, half-sitting, half-lying.
This was his last defiance to his approaching fate, and a
few hours later he surrendered himself to the great endless flood."

In his account of Harris's life, especially of his last thirty
years, it is evident that Kingsmill is all the time on guard
against the danger of his lapsing into sentimentality and con-
doning actions which, in a man he had not met and found to be
in some degree lovable, would have been dismissed with summary jurisdiction. The most severe strictures on Harris in the
second half of the book—that is after Harris's decline and
Kingsmill's first meeting with him—came not from the biographer at all, but are contained in two long letters, quoted
almost in full, from Mr. and Mrs. Buckland-Plummer, who
were associated with Harris during part of his disastrous editorship of *Pearson's Magazine* from 1916 to 1922. It is incon-

ceivable that in the case of a more successful man Kingsmill would have surrendered the initiative in such a manner. Middleton Murry, who considered the book clever but unsympathetic, may possibly have been irritated by the appearance of himself and of Katherine Mansfield as two of Harris's most ardent followers. The book indeed opens with a hilarious but poignant account of Harris reducing Murry to tears and mistaking Katherine Mansfield for a girl friend of Harold Weston's. "I suppose he [Murry] has not enjoyed the publicity given to his tears," Kingsmill reflected afterwards, "Yet Jesus wept, so he is in company of his own choosing."

Various other modern critics have followed Middleton Murry's example, using such words as "hostile", "malicious", and even "scrappy" to describe the writing. The task of elucidating its positive qualities is made no less difficult by the discordant sound of those who have sung its praises, *The Times* in 1949 asserting that it "ruthlessly shattered a never entirely secure legend," while *The Times Literary Supplement* in 1959 maintained that "it celebrated the legend most agreeably."

In reality Kingsmill had attempted to do something far more complex than either of these two interpretations suggest, to study what he had once admired in Harris and to disentangle with loving care what was of value in him from all the sound and fury of his life. Harris, like Kingsmill himself, passionately desired to be acclaimed by his contemporaries and remembered by posterity; like Kingsmill, too, he failed to achieve these ambitions. Though Kingsmill was fascinated by the spectacle of success he was always more sympathetically disposed towards the obscure than to those who impressed public opinion with their outbursts of altruistic sentiments. The facets in Harris's character which come in for gravest condemnation—his lust for power, his false rhetoric, his vanity and sentimentality—are all those which, by themselves, might have led him to attain his ultimate goal. The reckless exasperation which set at nought Harris's assiduously laid plans appealed to Kingsmill, in whom it answered a similar impatience. There was, too, a breath of fresh air about much of Harris's vehemence. "In a world where the powerful meet on all sides with the most exquisite consideration and courtesy," he wrote in *After Puritanism*, "a discord refreshes the ear wearied by the unbroken harmony. Such discords were, one fancies, introduced on most suitable occasions by Harris. . . ."

Kingsmill's approval of Harris's outspoken assertions, dictated not by political convenience but by an inner dissatisfaction, is clearly visible in his account of what may be taken as the turning point in Harris's career, the Parnell case.

"As a Conservative, he [Harris] was expected to use the scandal to Parnell's discredit. But sick of respectability, bored by his wife and her well-dressed friends, and provoked by the torrent of cant which was pouring over England, he went down to Hackney (his parliamentary constituency), attacked Gladstone as a hypocrite, and asserted that he was not prepared to go into battle against the Home Rulers with Kitty O'Shea's petticoat for a flag. The next day eighty members of the hundred on his committee resigned."

Rebecca West, Ivor Brown and Evelyn Waugh were among the more perceptive critics of Kingsmill's *Frank Harris*, but probably the best critic of all is Malcolm Muggeridge, who read it no less than six times (by 1951, that is) and commented thus :

"Again, as with Arnold, there is a note of genuine affection. The fact that Hughie saw through Harris so devastatingly did not prevent him from appreciating the touch of pathos, and even poetry, which lay in the fantastic disproportion between Harris's aspirations and performance. . . . He made, for instance, Harris's absurdity, his very lies and insincerities, seem no more than the poor accoutrements with which Don Quixote set forth mounted upon Rosinante."

Both Kingsmill and his publisher expected *Frank Harris* to become a best-seller, as indeed it should have done. Perhaps, though, it was published too soon after Harris's death. In any event Kingsmill was greatly disappointed over the comparatively small sales. "If one writes that the late Mr. B—— was full of private integrity and public zeal," he remarked after reading some of the reviews, "one is a good fellow. If one unravels the reasons which led the late Mr. B—— to qualify his private integrity with rape, and his public zeal with espionage, one is an Iago. It is all very disheartening. Nine critics out of ten have no idea that one may be interested in human character for its own sake."

While working on his *Frank Harris* at Thonon, Kingsmill had also been writing a series of parodies for *The Bookman* (New York) and *The English Review*, and in March 1933, shortly before he and his family returned to England, these parodies were published in a book, *The Table of Truth*. He had always enjoyed writing parodies which, if well done, he considered to be the most perfect form of criticism. His first printed parodies, on Hall Caine, Hilaire Belloc and G. K. Chesterton had appeared in *The Isis*, and others, among which were those on W. E. Henley, and Herbert Trench, had followed in *The Dawn's Delay*.

Unlike many parodies, Kingsmill's are penetrating rather than elaborate. That is to say that they do not merely seek to exaggerate certain often superficial tricks of style, but attempt to caricature something deeper—some salient aspects of character in the writer himself, which are reflected, often unconsciously, in his prose or verse. This fact accounts for the peculiar lack of conformity in overall opinion amongst the readers of the book, for some intimate understanding of the subject of the parody is needed to appreciate the subtlety of the writing. Thus, admirers of Browning have appreciated his *In a Charabanc* without finding any great merit in the H. G. Wells parody, while H. G. Wells's enthusiasts usually enjoy *A Word to Mr. Jones*, but may never raise a smile at the Browning

poem. Mr. R. G. G. Price finds the Wells parody unrecogniz-
able but Wells himself was appreciative, and after reading it
invited Kingsmill to tea, adding at the end of his letter, "You're
ALL RIGHT." But those with only scant knowledge of Kingsmill's
subjects, picked up merely from some existing legend surrounding them, may consequently be surprised by these parodies.
Those readers, for example, who have heard of Frank Harris
only as a pornographic autobiographer, will be disappointed
in Kingsmill's *Lewis Carroll. A Contemporary Portrait after
Frank Harris* at the exposition, for instance, of the pseudo-
mysticism of Harris's last days, which may appear unintelligible.

The highly individualistic style of Carlyle guaranteed Kingsmill a wider appreciation of his efforts, and his vigorous and
amusing remarks on *Some Modern Light Bringers* put into
Carlyle's mouth—among whose victims were Bernard Shaw,
Proust, Lytton Strachey and James Joyce—met with universal
approval. In at least two more of these parodies, those on P.
G. Wodehouse and A. E. Housman, where their peculiar and
easily recognizable style is fused inseparably with the whole
outlook and emotion of their author, the humour was readily
appreciated by all. The Housman parody, praised by Housman himself as the best ever written, has indeed become
famous, and is the only piece of writing which rivals *Invective
and Abuse* in general popularity and renown. Being short and
eminently quotable, it can be reproduced here as an example
of Kingsmill's ability as a parodist.

> "What, still alive at twenty-two,
> A clean upstanding lad like you?
> Sure, if your throat 'tis hard to slit,
> Slit your girl's, and swing for it.
>
> Like enough you won't be glad,
> When they come to hang you, lad :
> But bacon's not the only thing
> That's cured by hanging from a string.

So when the spilt ink of the night
Spreads o'er the blotting pad of light,
Lads whose job is still to do
Shall whet their knives, and think of you."

15

Johnson and Dickens

IN THE SPRING OF 1933, KINGSMILL BROUGHT HIS FAMILY BACK
to England to live at The Black Mill, Ore, Hastings, a con-
verted windmill, roomy, and romantically situated on the far
end of a hill looking out on open fields and the slate-blue sea
below. Here they all remained for the next three years. During
this period he reviewed books regularly for *The English Review*
and intermittently for *Time and Tide*, *The New Statesman*,
The Listener and *The Sunday Express*, and some six months
after his return to England, he completed his life of Samuel
Johnson.

Samuel Johnson is probably Kingsmill's best biography,
giving an intimate and human portrait of the man whom above
all others he had come to venerate. The writing in this book
is distinguished by great wisdom, much tenderness, and a deep
knowledge and understanding of human nature. Nothing
which does not directly relate to Johnson himself, and illustrate
some facet of his character is included; the beam of Kingsmill's critical observation and expert attention is always
focussed upon his subject. The style is clear and straightforward and there are many characteristically neat phrases ending
often with a subtle and unexpected antithesis. Of Lord Chester-
field's papers on the Dictionary, for example, he wrote "The
compliments he poured on Johnson had nothing sincere in
them except their note of condescension."

The only fault to be found with this biography, and one of
which Kingsmill became aware himself some years after it had
been published, is that his love of Johnson sometimes softened
the edge of his normally acute criticisms, so that his sympathy

in places outweighs his strict and balanced sense of reality. The view which Kingsmill held of Johnson, and which he successfully put over in his book was "of an essentially imaginative nature clogged by melancholia, a profound thinker limited by inborn and irrational fears, and an intensely loving and compassionate soul hampered in its expression by lifelong disabilities of mind and body." Though well received at the time, the book created no outrageous stir and was soon forgotten. Doubtless it was this neglect which persuaded Kingsmill to write in 1948 that he *inferred* from later studies that his portrait "has helped to modify the old John Bull conception and also to adjust the balance between Boswell and Mrs. Thrale."

As in the case of his anthology, *Johnson Without Boswell,* his object in this biography was to show the incompleteness of Boswell's *Life of Johnson* and to present an entirely different figure from the one made popular by Carlyle and Macaulay. With Charles Dickens, his next full length biographical subject, his adversary was Chesterton, whose portrait of that novelist as a philanthropic and selfless social worker considerably vexed him. This was the myth which he set out to attack, but it does not explain on its own the extreme and unrelieved severity which characterizes the book from first to last.

It has been suggested by Hesketh Pearson that Dickens strongly reminded Kingsmill of Sir Henry Lunn, with whom in the course of the book he became confused. Although there is some truth in this assertion, Sir Henry Lunn's influence over his son can easily be exaggerated and prolonged unduly. In 1928, a year after he had left the family business and when he was writing his *Matthew Arnold,* Kingsmill undoubtedly still felt extremely bitter against his father, and his own description of this book only four years later as "written, it may be, too much in the spirit of a young man chasing his great-grandfather round the garden with a pitchfork" indicates that he had already come to realize the parental nature of his onslaught upon Arnold. By 1934, the ardour of this personal animosity had greatly diminished, and we must look for another cause to account for his harassing pursuit of Dickens from page to page.

The reason seems to be not in Dickens's similarity to Sir Henry Lunn so much as to Kingsmill himself. This view is confirmed by the fact that he is far more virulent in attacking Dickens's sentimentality and its various offshoots such as morbidity than his snobbishness. To the outside world both Dickens and Kingsmill could present a front which effectively concealed all inner dissatisfactions and longings. Many of Kingsmill's friends have testified to his explosions of loud laughter and to his vivid and animated personality, and have consequently been somewhat surprised by the morbid tone of some of his fiction; and as shrewd an observer as Carlyle was deceived into thinking that Dickens went through life in a state of perennial good humour. But whereas Kingsmill found most frequent release to his suppressed emotionalism in repeatedly falling in love at first sight, Dickens discharged the full flow of his sentimentalism directly into his novels, which consequently for all their faults, retain the spirit of vitality of the author. Dickens's literary sentimentalism is therefore unabashed, whereas Kingsmill's, arising inevitably from the strong autobiographical nature of his novels, spurts and trickles in a thin uneven stream, reluctant and unintentional, the unsuccessful repression of which often makes the writing vapid and listless.

Many of the faults which Dickens paraded in his writing, Kingsmill kept buried within him. He accused Dickens of self-pity; and self-pity is displayed clearly in his own *Blondel*. Again, he censures Dickens's sentimentality; yet nearly all his own fiction shows that he was a sentimentalist at heart himself. He points out that the projection of Dickens's longings often excluded his sense of reality; but the projection of his own longings accounts for the frequent lack of objectivity in nearly all his own novels, especially *Blondel* and *The Fall*. Both of them were irritably and articulately excited by hostile criticism; both were highly susceptible to the physical appeal of women; both, finding it difficult to resist any chance of making money, and unwilling to see any point of view other than their own in financial matters, became involved in difficulties with a number of publishers.

The theme of *The Sentimental Journey*, the title he gave to this biography, shows that "that he [Dickens] had been cheated in life was his deepest and most constant emotion." Yet even here it is probable that Kingsmill feared his own feelings might easily degenerate into this state, for it is interesting to note that William Gerhardi, in his novel written round the character of Kingsmill, *Pending Heaven*, puts into his hero's mouth these words, which recur throughout the book with various delicate variations like some rhythmic theme from a Mozart symphony—"Unless one day I win that girl I shall be cheated out of what is best and most generous in life." The close similarity of these two themes, the one in Kingsmill's *The Sentimental Journey*, and the other in Gerhardi's *Pending Heaven*, is no accidental coincidence, but accurately mirrors Kingsmill's own similarity to Dickens.

"When my book on Johnson was nearly over, I dreamed that I was on the summit of a high mountain," he wrote many years later, "From a deep chasm far below came the subdued roar of a torrent, but I felt no fear. The snow around me shone in the light of the sun, and I was filled with a sense of liberation. Towards the close of my book on Dickens I dreamed that I was on the slope of a high range, a little below the crest. There were shifting patches of light on the snowfields near me, but I was conscious of the precipices beneath, and fear mingled with my relief."

To reduce this somewhat elevated passage to more manageable proportions, one might paraphrase it by saying that just as he found his similarity to Johnson most gratifying and was induced to take great trouble with the book to the extent of giving it a full index so his likeness to Dickens aggravated him and he read through only a synopsis of Dickens's works in preparation, wrote the book hastily and read through the proofs without attention. The word "relief" in the paragraph quoted above is quite out of harmony with the rest of the

passage, and gives a clue to his uppermost feelings as, chapter
by chapter, he hurried to the end of *The Sentimental Journey*.
With Johnson he had tended to identify himself with his subject and heighten his merits, but with Dickens he was at pains
to distinguish himself from his subject and so stressed his
defects.

The result of this hasty treatment is, that though the theme
of the book can hardly be disputed, Kingsmill often selected
inconclusive evidence to support his various contentions. On
a first reading, *The Sentimental Journey* strikes one as the
most consistently brilliant of all his biographies, but much of
this gloss is taken away by minor inaccuracies which appear
on the surface after it is examined closely. His innate fairness
of mind forbade him writing what he thought to be incorrect,
but he so often reiterates, with several nice variations of
emphasis, the same charges he brings against Dickens that the
overall effect is lop-sided. Often he would endeavour to praise
what he admired in Dickens, the humour of his minor characters or his wonderful powers of description, starting the sentence with a few words of approbation and then continuing,
to borrow the words which he himself applied to Frank Harris,
"with reservations which soon far outweighed the opening
eulogy."

Even after completing *The Sentimental Journey* he did not
succeed in working his spleen over Dickens out of his system,
and in his review of Thomas Wright's biography which came
out in the year after his own, he wrote his only work of criticism
which is blatantly and obviously unfair. He was at the time
irritated with Wright who had made use of some of the conclusions reached in his own book without any acknowledge-
ment. But to vent his anger and sense of personal injustice on
Dickens in a manner likely to bring harm only to himself is
no solution to a state of affairs which will persist so long as
biography is written.

Despite these shortcomings, *The Sentimental Journey* contains some brilliant writing and made a number of completely

original discoveries concerning Dickens—many of which have been embodied into the work of later critics as their personal contributions to Dickensian literary criticism. The most successful of such critics was probably Edmund Wilson, who simultaneously disparaged Kingsmill at the beginning of his essay "Dickens: The Two Scrooges" which appeared in his seven studies in literature entitled *The Wound and the Bow*. Commenting on the collection a few years after its publication, Kingsmill wrote, "The book bristled with ideas which, though momentarily stimulating, had the peculiar emptiness of ideas evolving out of one another instead of growing out of experience. There seemed to be little connection between Mr. Wilson's brilliant mental apparatus and the rest of Mr. Wilson. This state of disassociation being common at present, the book had a great success in the States and here, and was especially appreciated by the many persons nowadays addicted to the game of Hunt the Symbol."

Since, with the possible exception of Kipling, he could hardly have been given a more unfortunate subject for a best-seller, several of the reviews were far from flattering. Many of the critics were side-tracked into displaying their own Dickensian scholarship by pointing out minor inaccuracies (though there are fewer of these than has been supposed), while others contented themselves with an outburst or two of moral indignation against his treatment of the Ellen Ternan affair. Both types of criticism are worth examining.

In the course of his criticism of *A Tale of Two Cities*, Kingsmill describes Mr. Stryver as "a disreputable solicitor", a slip due perhaps to an unconscious prejudice in favour of barristers as compared with solicitors. But the critic who challenged him to produce evidence that Mr. Hannibal Chollop was a major could have found him referred to as such when he replies to Mark Tapley's designation of Eden as a swamp. Nor was he entirely incorrect, as has been suggested, in presuming Mr. Jarndyce was a merchant. Admittedly, it is not directly stated that he was a retired merchant by Dickens, who is equally vague concerning the details of the Jarndyce and Jarndyce case. But that Mr. Jarndyce had been in business is, as Kingsmill would put it, "obvious" when his general tone and attitude are compared to the tone and attitude assigned by Dickens to the genuine country gentleman, Sir Leicester Dedlock. His eager partiality to generalization is yet another sign of the haste with which the book was written. "There are many thrashings in Dickens," he writes, "there are many intimidations of the vile by the virtuous, but there are no fights." It is true that there are a preponderance of thrashings to more evenly matched contests; Squeers is beaten by Nicolas Nickleby without opposing resistance, as is Noah Claypole by Oliver Twist. Pecksniff, too, as Kingsmill points out, "providentially falls backwards over a chair" before Martin Chuzzlewit can come to grips with him. But what about Miss Pross and Madam Defarge in *A Tale of Two Cities*? Or Rogue Riderhood and Bradley Headstone in *Our Mutual Friend*? Or the encounter with the butcher in *David Copperfield*? Or Sam Weller and the other specials in *The Pickwick Papers*? Or Mulberry Hawks and Nicolas Nickleby? Or again Helena Landless and Edwin Drood? It is possible that Kingsmill could have disqualified at least some of these as examples of genuine fights, but his unbroken silence regarding them is disconcerting.

One of the most recent and serious critics of *The Sentimental Journey* is Mr. K. J. Fielding, himself the author of a book of Dickens and an associate editor of the definitive edition of Dickens's letters. As Mr. Fielding indicates in a popular monograph on Dickens which he wrote for The British Council, there is a lapse in Kingsmill's usual stylistic precision verging on contradiction when he comes to classify the importance of Ellen Ternan in Dickens's life. But this is again due to the haste in which he wrote the book and not to any wavering inconclusion on his part. There is, in fact, no major contradiction in what he writes. In a note at the beginning of *The Sentimental Journey* he referred to Thomas Wright's narrative of Dickens's relations with Ellen Ternan which appeared on

April 3rd 1934 in *The Daily Express* as "the most important contribution to the biography of Dickens in this century." Again, at the end of his book, he states that "though Ellen Ternan appealed at first to his [Dickens's] idealism she soon became the object of the sensuality with which he tried to drug the unhappiness of his later years." In *The Progress of a Biographer*, which Mr. Fielding does not quote, Kingsmill also wrote : "Dickens's affair with Ellen Ternan, the details of which appeared shortly after I began my book, did not take up much space in the narrative, or seem to me of essential importance; for Dickens to me was a child who never grew up, with the genius of a child and its intense egotism, natural and fruitful in the giving of life but corroding and destructive in later years."

This statement, though it certainly modifies the original note at the beginning of *The Sentimental Journey* contradicts Mr. Fielding's conclusion that the biography "suffers from the method of coming to conclusions first and finding reasons afterwards."

Mr. Fielding gives two more illustrations designed to strengthen this conclusion. First, he writes that "in order to support his contention that Dickens preferred Wilkie Collins's friendship and was contemptuous of Forster as early as 1858, he [Kingsmill] inferred that a remark about 'solemn impostors' in one of Dickens's letters to Collins was intended to apply to Forster because of his opposition to public readings; yet a brief investigation would have shown that it referred to members of the committee of a literary society with whom Dickens, supported by Forster, was engaged in controversy." Such an inaccuracy, Mr. Fielding concludes, matters in principle, since Dickens could never have written such a phrase in 1858, and therefore the mistake shows a fundamental misunderstanding of Dickens's character.

Mr. Fielding is more accurate in his facts than imaginative in the conclusions he draws from them. A mis-reading of detail is not the same as a basic misinterpretation of character, and it is far-fetched indeed to maintain that Dickens was incapable of forming the phrase "solemn impostors" in 1858 as referring to a committee of solemn impostors—whoever else he may have had in mind when he wrote it. Moreover, Mr. Fielding has himself misread Kingsmill which, applying his own sweeping conclusion, should exonerate one from considering his view on *The Sentimental Journey*. There is no suggestion that Dickens was "contemptuous" of Forster. In Chapter V (page 148) Kingsmill wrote : "when the novel [*Bleak House*] was finished he went for a holiday in Switzerland and Italy with Wilkie Collins, whom he had met while acting. Wilkie Collins who was not yet thirty, became from this time on Dickens's favourite companion. Forster had been invaluable to Dickens while he was making his way, socially and as a writer. Now that he was established, and sick of the prison into which he had broken, Dickens turned with relief to the pleasure-loving Collins. There was no break between him and Forster, but he no longer used Forster as the confidant of all his plans. Forster's consequential manner had often annoyed him in the past, and he now worked off some of his annoyance by making fun of Forster with Collins. "Forster," he wrote Collins a year or two after they first met, "doesn't seem to be managing Sebastopol as well as I expected of him. I thought he would have stormed the place before now."

The sentence containing the phrase "solemn impostors" occurs some forty pages later, in the final chapter of the book. The only place other than the passage quoted from Chapter V in which Dickens's association with Collins and Forster enters the narrative is one sentence at the beginning of the penultimate chapter (page 161).

"A few pages later," Mr. Fielding continues, "in order to substantiate his assertion that Dickens showed an obvious 'mental and moral determination' after about 1867, he cited an incident which was supposed to have taken place in 1868 but which his source clearly shows to have happened some time in the 'forties." But Kingsmill in fact did no such thing. He examined the essays appearing in *The Uncommercial Traveller* which often dealt with incidents which had occurred some years back in Dickens's life, but which were written between 1861 and Dickens's death in 1870, and whose peculiar quality undoubtedly belongs to the period 1858-1870 in which Kingsmill has placed them.

Since his life of Johnson was so soon forgotten, and his studies of Arnold and Dickens excited, for the most part, much hostile criticism, Kingsmill was by now established in the minds of most critics and the reading public as an iconoclastic critic and debunking biographer.

16

The Collaborator

IN THE SAME YEAR AS THE PUBLICATION OF *The Sentimental Journey* Kingsmill embarked upon his first collaboration, bringing out *The Casanova Fable* with William Gerhardi in 1934. His treatment of Casanova illustrates what had been evident even in his days as editor of *The Isis*—that he had always to write against some existing conception, preferably popular at the time. His attack on Chesterton's portrait of Dickens has already been noted. In the case of Casanova he wrote against Havelock Ellis's picture of him as "a free spirit, a wit and bold thinker." This technique of writing is clearly discernible in his other books also. With Johnson he had tried to demolish the John Bull fable; with Arnold, the myth of the sexless academic. And in future years he was to inveigh against the virgin-queen conception of Elizabeth, and in the case of Cromwell dispute the contention, widely held during the war years, that he was the greatest of all Englishmen past and present.

The Casanova Fable is divided into two separate sections. The first and longest of these, called "The Evidence," consists of a concise and straightforward biography written by Kingsmill, while the second, "The Summing Up," is a more complex but entertaining dialectical essay by William Gerhardi. The original suggestion of a book on Casanova had come from Hutchinson's, the publishers, and was extended to William Gerhardi alone. He, in turn, discussed the idea with Kingsmill who soon grew enthusiastic over the prospect of the unavoidable financial success, as he saw it, of a collaboration. But the publishers proved less enthusiastic towards Kingsmill's idea than their own, no doubt wishing that Gerhardi could have seen fit to choose a more eminent and august co-author. Eventually they agreed to the joint plan under the stipulation that Kingsmill's name should appear second to Gerhardi's on the cover of the book. This caused no violent objections, and Kingsmill hastened away to complete what amounts to nearly three-quarters of the book all in the space of a few weeks, fully convinced that now at last he was on to a best-seller.

That Kingsmill possessed little admiration or interest in Casanova as a man or a writer can be clearly seen from a critical essay he wrote in the spring of the previous year on the publication of Mr. Bonamy Dobrée's study of Casanova. "There is nothing of intrinsic value in Casanova's *Memoirs*," he wrote, "no sense of character, no humour or thought. What interest they have is accidental and independent of the narrator's own intention. He has drawn his own portrait, but between the lines. He is amusing but not when he wishes to be. He traverses life without converting any experience into his own possession, and instead of creating his own world tries to break into the worlds of others."

Kingsmill's short biography is preceded by an introduction which considers the veracity of Casanova's *Memoirs*, concluding that "he seldom suppresses or transforms his actions in the interests of his moral reputation, but contents himself with denying that they were as reprehensible as an intelligent person might suppose. His memoirs, to sum up, are not misleading through failing to reveal what he did, but through the addition of imaginary embellishments. Casanova, had he quarrelled with a prostitute, knocked her down, and gone off with her purse, would have narrated the incident without a qualm, but a vague feeling that a little glamour was needed to round the story off would have made him introduce a lovely young countess designed by art and nature to make a man forget the small unpleasantnesses of life."

The tone of his biographical writing on Casanova Kingsmill described as "mildly sceptical." Sceptical it certainly is, though some might question the "mildly" once he had got underweigh in applying himself to the man whose gratification of his own senses "was only less important . . . than the gratification of his vanity," and who, "though of immense importance to himself," failed to achieve any noteworthy distinction in action or in literature.

Kingsmill thought of this book as a by-product of his study on Harris, and his investigations into Harris's character three years before helped him to trace the course of Casanova's life and to shorten the time he spent on this task. The book though does not bear comparison with his *Frank Harris*, since the motive for writing it was entirely different. But that the two months spent altogether over it were justifiable, his creditors, he remarked, were the first to realize. On the other hand it is doubtful whether he would have considered worthwhile any further duration of time devoted to the "life of poor Casanova, the hero of those sprightly academics who spend their lives letting *I dare not* wait upon *In any case I couldn't.*"

This last remark, together with the title of the book, reveals the only aspect of Casanova which Kingsmill really found intriguing—the disparity between the published *Memoirs* and available information, and the various and conflicting myths which under the persuasion of Schnitzler, Mr. Guy Endore and others had arisen around his life and character.

Two years after the publication of *The Casanova Fable*, in 1936, there appeared the first of two books of newspaper parodies which Kingsmill wrote in collaboration with Malcolm Muggeridge. *Brave Old World*, as this first one was called, gave both authors a vehicle for expressing their "sense of the ludicrousness of the times and the pomposity and foolishness of commentators upon them" by taking off many of the current journalistic forms from leading articles to gossip columns. "Supposing," the dust-jacket announced in letters capital and scarlet, "Othello were an English Colonial Governor, how would his career and its unfortunate end be treated by *The Times*, Dean Inge, Mr. James Douglas and Mr. J. L. Garvin?" And again,

"Supposing Mr. Ramsay Macdonald were found wandering on Hampstead Heath, unable to give a clear account of himself, would it make any difference?" These and many other questions were examined and answered in the course of the book which endeavoured to show that if most things were different, most things, especially the Press, would still be the same.

The authors themselves probably derived more enjoyment from compiling this book than most of their public got from reading it, for the readers would be unlikely to take any paper they found ridiculous, or to appreciate many of the parodies of papers they never ordered regularly. Although some of the items are quite amusing, there is little object in caricaturing the Press in general, for all newspapers contain their own parodies and those who see nothing funny in them will never appreciate such a book; while those who are amused are already supplied with a never-ending and daily source of such humour.

But while writing these parodies Kingsmill would temporarily forget his own financial predicament, and released from such worries, become expansive and carefree, radiating, as Malcolm Muggeridge wrote "a sense of happiness, of serenity, greater than any I have known." Together they would work with spasmodic leisureliness through the afternoons, Kingsmill lying on the sofa, Muggeridge making notes, and both of them ceasing from these exertions to have tea, or go for a walk or just simply to talk, until, to their surprise, they would see the afternoon light fade and recede from the sky and watch the evening come down, the dusk deepen into twilight; and another day was gone.

Possibly the best parody in the book, and one of which good use was made only recently by Anthony Howard, is that on "Peterborough" of *The Daily Telegraph*. The last paragraph runs as follows:

Ready and Kindly Wit

He [the Sultan of Turkey] has a ready and kindly wit, which has served him well on occasion. Once, when he was

walking through the outskirts of Constantinople, he
noticed some men at work on the road. It was a hot afternoon and he remarked to the nearest :
'Warm work, eh?'
The workman laughingly assented.

Both *Brave Old World* and the second book together, *Next
Year's News*, are illustrated with a series of amusing cartoons
by Sidney Maiden. *Next Year's News*, published in 1938, is
similar to their early collaboration. Many of the items, Anthony
Eden's Questionnaire, the Court Circular, or Peter Fleming's
History of Eton, for example, seem to the impartial reader
only fractionally exaggerated. Among the more humorous
ideas is the ceremonial presentation of an honorary degree by
Cambridge University to Sir Tweed Harris, whose family have
been connected for several generations with the manufacture
of Cambridge sausages. Later in the same year Sir Tweed,
who, it was reported, was in the process of donating a large
amount of money by instalments to the Cambridge University
Million Pounds Appeal, was again honoured by that establishment which conferred upon him the Edward VII Gold Medal
for "single proficiency in the ancient tongues, or an original
contribution to the mathematical or physical science, or for
acts tending to the furtherance of the same."
Another amusing item was the message sent by King George
that year to Hitler.

"The Queen and I, Your Excellency, are following with
interest the celebrations now taking place throughout Germany in connection with the tri-millenary of a venerable
figure belonging to the dawn of your great history. It is our
conviction that such celebrations, by drawing attention
to our common European heritage, cannot but serve the
cause of peace, which we all have at heart."

Neither *Brave Old World* nor *Next Year's News* sold particularly well, and Kingsmill, who had foreseen a rather different reception, went so far as to suggest that their publisher

should advertise as follows: "According to the authors, who appear to have private information, *Brave Old World* is in wild demand."

Apart from these two collaborations, Kingsmill and Muggeridge embarked upon another joint enterprise early in 1936. With the intention of starting up a new humorous weekly, they inserted in the personal columns of *The Times* the following advertisement:

A GROUP OF WRITERS *who believe that there is room for a weekly which would deal wittily and honestly with the modern world would be glad to hear from anyone interested in financing such a venture.*

This announcement having duly appeared they both waited with a mixture of excitement and sublime confidence for the flood of letters from the numerous men of affluence, who, they felt sure, would hasten to support so sensible a scheme. They received in all some five replies.

The first of these came from a man signing himself, "Jacob Berlin." An inmate from a House for Indigents in North London, he began by regretting that he would be unable to help the "group of writers" on the financial side. But, he continued, he had only the previous evening found occasion to remark to a young friend that though the English might not be religious they looked on Christ as the highest type of man, and were always hoping that he might come true. From this remark, he added, they would, as literary men themselves, be able to judge his capacity for combining wit with honesty—a talent which he earnestly assured them was at their disposal for the normal fees should their scheme materialize.

A second person wrote from Cardiff to say that if they would forward £25, he would proceed to float a company for them, intending to raise about £1,000 to £2,000 by means of debentures. He would, he added, be delighted to forward them computations showing how the original amount of £25 was arrived at. But this man, unlike their first correspondent, made no claim to be honest, and both Kingsmill and Muggeridge on their side felt that humour rather than wit was the strong point. A third reply came from a person who asked for further details of their scheme. They answered promptly, inviting him to the Authors' Club one afternoon, and adding that he need not reply if the time proved suitable. He neither troubled to reply nor to appear.

In another letter from Zurich much generous appreciation was expressed for the project, but the writer went on to suggest that they form themselves into a company "the way people do who make potato chips, or soap or substitute butter," and that he himself might be persuaded to buy a few of their shares, always providing that the price was fixed conveniently low. He would in any case like to keep in touch with them, he continued, since should he ever own a newspaper in London himself, he would need witty and honest writers.

Their last answer came from a publisher of a badminton magazine, whom with some difficulty they sought out in the purlieus of Westminister. The publisher in question was at pains to emphasize that he dealt only in papers which had a ready-made public, and was disappointed to learn that it was impossible to forecast in what towns and districts of England honesty and wit would be most acceptable.

Despairing at length of any suitable correspondence, the two friends approached a theatrical agent, whose appreciation of their difficulties proved large and warm-hearted, but who couched his generalizations in terms which, though genial and even impressive, remained unspecific.

After this the project was finally abandoned.

Besides his collaborations with William Gerhardi and Malcolm Muggeridge, Kingsmill wrote three "talk and travel" books with Hesketh Pearson. In 1937, the year after Boswell's Original Journal of the *Tour of the Hebrides* was first published, Kingsmill and Pearson set out on a pilgrimage in the steps of their predecessors, and not wishing to keep secret a full record of their experiences for a century or more, published them in an unexpurgated form, *Skye High*, a lively account of their journey together. "Johnson and Boswell travelled in glory and discomfort," Kingsmill remarked as they started, "we expect to travel in comfort but much less glory. However, in imitation of our predecessors, we shall endeavour to be entertained *en route* by learned professors and an unwary laird or two."

Skye High is readable and quite entertaining, and it gives some idea of Kingsmill's powers as a conversationalist and wit even though a number of the discussions and incidents recorded were formalized so that they lack some of the initial pungency and spontaneity of the original direct speech. Despite much vitality and humour, the writing is not entirely free from self-consciousness, a characteristic which becomes less apparent in their later collaborations. In all three of their joint books, it is interesting to distinguish between Kingsmill's definite but reasoned voice, and the more dogmatic assertiveness of Pearson, a literary mannerism which he "has spent my life attempting to subdue," and the stubborn persistence of which has concealed from his less percipient critics an essentially warm and sympathetic temperament.

One of the objects of *Skye High* was to reconstruct Johnson and Boswell at certain places on their route through Scotland. "Another of our objects," Hesketh Pearson wrote in his reminiscences, *Thinking it Over*, "was to enjoy ourselves. . . . But when two authors write to please themselves they cannot expect to please everyone else." Kingsmill, on the other hand, believed that the only way to write a successful book was to forget all about his prospective audience. Although enthusiastically received by David Garnett, Harold Nicolson and Evelyn Waugh, the book was not a commercial success, for it could only appeal to that minority of genuine readers of literature who appreciate the page they are in the process of reading and do not, like most people, hurry through the lines of print before them with an anxious impatience to find out with the least possible delay what is on the following page.

Despite past experience there is no evidence to suggest that Kingsmill was at any time anticipating anything less than a best-seller. Like many uncalculating men of genius he was entirely unrealistic as to his personal prospects of financial success. "I am optimistic," he once said, "about everything I cannot control, and as I can control practically nothing I am optimistic about practically everything." At first unable to account for the lack of sales, he soon laid the blame at the door of his publisher, Hamish Hamilton, whom he accused of putting the ridiculously high price of twelve shillings and sixpence on the book, due to his fear of losing too much money through his and Pearson's efforts.

Sobered perhaps by the reception and sales of their first joint book, their next collaboration was not produced until five years later. The first vague premonition of it came to them as early as January 1939, at which time they went for a few days together first to Marlborough and then to the Cotswolds. The moment had now arrived, they felt, for them to follow any Englishman whom they could pursue not too assiduously through England and who, at the same time, was sufficiently in the public eye to arouse the interest and stimulate the generosity of Hamish Hamilton. At the interview which preceded their trip they outlined their plan. "Hesketh has never been to Marlborough," Kingsmill explained to Hamish Hamilton, "so that is to be our starting place. We are just going to wander about that part of the world, drifting gradually towards Stratford and piecing Shakespeare together as we go."

Two years later, still without a publisher, Kingsmill expressed in slightly more coherent language the same vagueness of outline. "We can start with our Cotswold journey," he told Pearson, "and then proceed with no settled plan. It would be un-English to deal with our subject systematically. As we are both English, it is reasonable to assume that England will emerge from the book. I do not say the whole of England but much more than if we were both French. It will be a book from which a sensitive reader will be able to infer England. That gets it. *Infer* England."

Eventually Methuen's agreed to publish their book. Over lunch with Alan White first Kingsmill and then Pearson found difficulty in conveying anything in particular about it, and were at last forced back into repeating a number of times that it would be "a book from which a sensitive reader will be able to *infer* England." By the end of the meal though, everything was settled, even the title, *This Blessed Plot*, which seems to have recommended itself largely on the grounds of ambiguity, Kingsmill expressing the fervent hope that it would ensnare the readers of thrillers who, even by the last page, he guaranteed would be unable to detect the plot in question.

Though lacking the more obvious thread which ran through *Skye High*, *This Blessed Plot* is an improvement on their first collaboration. There are a number of amusing stories, autobiographical and otherwise, and some witty observations. Kingsmill's conversation was not, like that of Oscar Wilde, studied with clever paradox and epigrammatic repartee, but there was a humorous flavour to everything he said. When talking he was never artificial and ideas flowed effortlessly from him, everyone, incidentally, seeming to have been "old man"— even his daughters. Even his dreams, were funny. "A somewhat acid wench was talking to me, at a dinner party, in a polished tone," he reported one dream to Pearson, "I listened for what appeared to be ten minutes, and then, leaning across the table and wagging my finger at her, said : 'One word—and one word only—Tripe!' Immense applause all round the table."

Many of his maxims and aphorisms were shrewdly realistic rather than superficially clever, as a number of examples taken from his conversation and writings will show :

"Things always turn out worse than one hopes and better than one imagines."

"Disillusionment is the result of discovering that other people are as egotistical as oneself."

"Pleasure is only pleasurable when a man is happy, but otherwise is only a distraction from pain."

"When thieves fall out another lot falls in."

"Verse is a form of expression in which an English writer can say almost anything he likes, without much risk of being detected."

"Spiritualism is the mysticism of the materialist."

"Society is based on the assumption that everyone is alike and no one is alive."

"It is as much a form of credulity to believe nothing as to believe everything."

The generalizations which spring from his family relations and his lack of literary recognition sometimes have a more bitter note to them. For instance :

"Friends are God's apology for relations."

"The law of libel is operative everywhere except in a court of law."

"A gentleman has all the qualities of a saint, except saintliness."

"Charity may cover a multitude of sins, but success transmits them into virtues."

"It is difficult to love mankind unless one has a reasonable private income, and when one has a reasonable private income one has better things to do than loving mankind."

His comments, too, on various writers could be pungent and amusing. Byron was "the most energetic and successful of all publicity agents," Oliver Wendell Holmes he described as "a mid-Victorian Sterne, whose amorousness exhales in innocent archness and idealization." Of Frank Harris he remarked, "he has a heart of borrowed gold." And H. G. Wells was a "Janus-faced little man . . . one of those pied pipers whom the Victorians followed out of this world into the world of today," while his *Short History of the World* he once described as

"Omniscience without Tears." Contrasting D. H. Lawrence's *Women in Love* with *The Plumed Serpent* he wrote: "The difference in verisimilitude [is] only such as might exist between one of Tennyson's *Idylls of the King* rewritten in a mad house by Dostoievsky and Rider Haggard's *She* transposed by Nietzsche into the style of *Also Sprach Zarathrustra*."

Kingsmill's third collaboration with Hesketh Pearson, which was published in 1947, was originally intended by the publisher to be the text, supplied by Pearson alone, to a number of drawings of London by Marjory Whittington. This was the plan early in 1944, but by the spring of the following year Pearson's contribution had been transformed into a proposed third talk and travel book on the Home Counties. At intervals during the next two years Douglas Jerrold, who, as the publisher, was by no means easy in his mind at the way things were shaping, would meet Kingsmill and Pearson and endeavour to find out whether their text in any way conformed to Marjory Whittington's drawings; and it is possible that he was none too pleased at the final result.

But *Talking of Dick Whittington*, another title, incidentally, which confined no one to anything, is the best of the three talk and travel books. Besides the usual stories the book contains interesting interviews with Hilaire Belloc, Lord Baldwin, A. E. W. Mason and Bernard Shaw. But throughout their talks and travels it is Pearson who seems in the ascendent, while Kingsmill appears to be more tired than before, drained of his usual exuberance and energy. Possibly due to this, the book is generally more mellow than their previous collaborations and the critics were at last more receptive, no longer comparing them, unfavourably, for the most part, with Sterne, Boswell, Peacock, Butler and Belloc.

The review which pleased both Kingsmill and Pearson most of all was one which appeared in the *Manchester Guardian* stating that they had invented the conversation travel book as a new art form. A friend of the present writer has written a parody of their first collaboration under the title *Hi Skye,* which high-lights its shortcomings as a novel work of art. One sentence of this parody runs : "We arrived that evening at the small hamlet of Elgol and laughed so much at one of Holroyd's remarks about Kingsmill that we were unable to eat dinner."

Prose has been defined as "a long intimacy between strangers." The partial failure of these talk and travel series is that they are only an intimate conversation between friends, with the reader half overhearing what is going on. He listens to the bursts of loud laughter, strains forward, but cannot quite catch everything that is being said, cannot account for the orgy of merriment. The mood of sustained euphoria in these books is undeniably an enviable state for the authors, but one which has its drawbacks for readers who cannot immediately share their elation. A completely successful work of art conveys as much to the reader as the author has put into it. "If only we could have made our readers laugh as frequently and heartily as we did," Hesketh Pearson wrote, "the sales of *Pickwick Papers* a century earlier would have lagged behind ours."

Since none of these collaborations brought Kingsmill very much money; since they involved him spending, for the most part, even more time away from his family than usual; since it could not be claimed that he was producing work which was too far ahead of his own age to qualify for recognition or reward, there were a number of people who deplored his spending time on such trivial activities. Among this number one may include his wife. Kingsmill was certainly aware of her feelings on this subject, and it was no doubt to appease her to some extent that before his trip with Pearson to the Cotswolds he called on Bernard Shaw and borrowed ten pounds from him on what he called "a preposterous errand."

But those who criticized Kingsmill's collaborations on the grounds that he should have occupied his time with more earnest and elevated compositions failed perhaps to appreciate his complete nature. Neither William Gerhardi, Malcolm Muggeridge nor Hesketh Pearson would presumably suggest that his books with them were of paramount literary importance or came near to being either his best or their own. Kingsmill's object of writing all of them had been to make some money and to enjoy himself, and had he been as successful in the former aim as in the latter, more people would doubtless have been reconciled to his efforts.

Kingsmill was a mystic, and it might seem strange to some that he devoted time to books of conversation, newspaper parodies or an account of Casanova's adventures. But he was the mystic who had criticized Blake for not having enough earth in him, and though his own head was often in the clouds his feet were always fixed firmly on the ground. "Life is so exciting and interesting," he once said, "that I mean to enjoy it while I am here, and my enjoyment is all the stronger for the sense of a perfect world beyond our reach and knowledge, but not beyond our occasional perception, while we are here. I hope to arrive in it some day in some form or other; but while here I mean to *be* here."

17

"D. H. Lawrence"

DURING THE YEAR 1936 KINGSMILL MOVED WITH HIS FAMILY to 24 Laton Road, Hastings, where he described his material state as laughable and his spasmodic visits to London as "crudely financial in intention, and crudely unfinancial in results."

To help alleviate this position he undertook translating a German novel into English. He seems to have possessed a considerable talent for translation, and was especially fond of translating German poetry. At Oxford, he had translated some Heine for *The Isis*, and after the war he occasionally translated other poems, usually for his own pleasure. One of Heine's poems, a wonderful description of his first love Amalie Heine's home by the North Sea, which Kingsmill translated in 1919, but which he never published, may be given here as an example of his ability in this field. The poem, written on Heine's "mattress-grave" at the end of his life, is called *Affrontenburg* (The Castle of Insults).

> "Nor in that garden anywhere
>   Could I find out one sheltering tree,
>   Where delicate tongues and brutal tongues
>   Could not pursue and torture me.
>
>   The toad that lurked within the grass
>   Informed the rat of all that passed,
>   And Viper had it presently,
>   And so to cousin frog at last.

Thus the whole filthy brood was primed
  With all I suffered every day.
Of all the insults that I bore,
  Never an item went astray.

How beautiful the roses bloomed,
  How sweet the fragrance which they shed.
But long before their hour they drooped
  Of a mysterious poison dead.

Since then the glorious nightingale
  Has sickened, too, and ceased in death.
The roses and their lover's song
  Were withered by the self-same breath.

Accursed garden! Yes, it seemed
  As though a curse were brooding there
Sometimes in the broad light of noon
  I shuddered with a phantom fear.

A green ghost grinned between the trees
  It was at me, at me he mocked!
And with an awful agony
  The bushes all about me rocked."

Apart from by translation, Kingsmill supplemented his income by occasional lectures, and in 1936 he delivered a series
of twelve such lectures at Ashford, at three pounds each.
Although a brilliant conversationalist, he proved to be a
remarkably bad lecturer, preferring to address his audience
from a chair in a low and mumbling murmur. Occasionally, if
the chairman was to protest, he would be induced to compromise, rising reluctantly to his feet and standing with knees
bent, his arms supporting his sagging body with such hopeless
lethargy that, as often as not, he was soon begged to resume
his seat once more. Once reseated, he would proceed to deliver
a "fireside talk" as one newspaper described it, speaking when-

ever possible about his personal friends—Edwin Muir, Kenneth Hare, William Gerhardi and others—whom he referred to by their Christian names.

A year after moving to Laton Road, Kingsmill began his study of D. H. Lawrence—a work that can have done little to dispel the established misconception of his writing. Once again the subject was unsuitable, and the prospect of undertaking such a book depressed him from the start. One cannot help wishing that he could have been allowed to write on people to whom he was more sympathetically disposed, such as Wordsworth or Blake.

While working on the biography of Lawrence, he called on Jessie Chambers, Lawrence's first love whom he portrayed as Miriam in *Sons and Lovers*, who was living with her husband in Lincolnshire. "A very remarkable woman indeed," he said afterwards, "but grim. She gave me the strong impression that she didn't relish strangers butting in on D. H. L. I was—need I say?—tact itself, until I got carried away when, referring to Lawrence's Mexico trip, I said, 'But you must read Mabel Luhan—you'll roar over it.' I need hardly say that Miriam is not in the happiest circumstances a roarer. Her expression pulled me up short. A painful moment."

While Kingsmill believed Lawrence to be a genius, he considered that his writing for the most part was unsatisfactory. The biography's inadequacy lies in Kingsmill's reluctance to linger for any length of time upon the positive nature and quality of Lawrence's genius. He was unfair, too, in that he suppressed some of the more genial sides of Lawrence's character which, however fleetingly they may have been indulged, would have weakened the impression he wished to create. Both David Garnett and Aldous Huxley had testified before the appearance of Kingsmill's study to Lawrence's humanity and generosity, but though there is much evidence presented as to his meanness and almost hysterical selfishness, Garnett's and Huxley's views are never mentioned.

The adolescent romanticism and biologico-mysticism of

Lawrence failed to attract Kingsmill, to whom they appeared at times like some parody of his own beliefs, while Lawrence's outbursts of irritation excited on occasion similar outbursts on Kingsmill's part. Much of his natural antipathy to Lawrence is apparent in such a revealing passage as: "Much mothered children soon attract support and encouragement. It is natural to provide a leaning wall with a prop. Cervantes and Johnson passed most of their lives in struggle and obscurity; Barrie and Kipling were famous in their middle twenties, and Lawrence, though too peculiar to become universally popular, was helped in one way and another throughout his career."

In addition to this, the unqualified materialistic creed of Lawrence's last days can hardly have failed to exasperate Kingsmill. Anyone reading this biography who beforehand had known nothing of Lawrence might well finish the book with the unshakable conviction that Lawrence was a first-class customer for some preventative home dealing primarily with advanced cases of lunacy. Lawrence's antics in various parts of the world filled Kingsmill with astonished wonder, and except for the first chapter and a half of the last, Lawrence's farcical activities are recounted for the most part with a half-incredulous and wholly entertaining brand of humour, which is raised to the pitch of pantomime when dealing with Lawrence's visit to Taos near the end of the book in a hilarious chapter entitled "Taotic."

There is no doubt that this biography, above all his others, which would have benefited also to a lesser extent, should have been lavishly illustrated by Max Beerbohm. The tale, as it unfolds, of Lawrence lumbering about the earth, pursued alternately by lumbering disciples and detectives, becomes so improbable that Kingsmill seems barely in control of his subject matter. Without doubt he employed considerable care in selecting the most fatuous statements from the four women who wrote on Lawrence—that is excluding "Miriam," Lawrence's early love—and when asked by his publisher whether he could not dispense with one of his more exaggerated quotations, he replied, "I would lose that with very real regret." In consequence much of the coldness extended towards the book is hardly surprising, for, as Mr. Armine Arnold has explained in his *D. H. Lawrence and America*, Kingsmill's portrait together with William York Tindall's study which appeared in the following year, "to a great extent managed to throw Lawrence off the literary stage, the one [Tindall's] for the literati, the other for the public." Describing the book as a salutary "cold douche" which was most enjoyable and, at the same time, necessary in reducing the inflamed reputation of Lawrence, Mr. Cyril Connolly wrote in *The New Statesman:*

> "For the first time the life of Lawrence has been subjected to a critical Johnsonian scrutiny, and with devastating effect."

Many of Lawrence's most gifted and interesting friends, some of whom Kingsmill himself had met, are sketched in the book—Middleton Murry, Aldous Huxley, Katherine Mansfield, Philip Heseltine ("Peter Warlock") and others. Middleton Murry is treated the most fully of all these, though, after being shown at the feet of Frank Harris some years earlier, he could probably have dispensed with Kingsmill's account of his temperamental relationship with Lawrence. Mr. Anthony Alpers, in his biography of Katherine Mansfield, has stated that Kingsmill was not detached where Murry was concerned. He gives no reason for the opinion, nor does there seem very much evidence to support it in the relevant passages in this book. For while Kingsmill's portrait of Murry is in places severe, it is not excessive and contains tributes to Murry's sincerity, imaginative insight and intellectual power.

It is probable that Mr. Alpers is merely quoting Murry's own opinion. Murry and Kingsmill saw each other fairly frequently in the days of *Hearth and Home* in which Kingsmill wrote a congratulatory article—quoted by Mr. Alpers—on Murry and Katherine Mansfield as joint editors of *Rhythm*. In August 1914 Kingsmill, accompanied by Douglas Jarrold, called on Murry to suggest that he should accompany them and enlist in a cyclist battalion at Putney. "He had discovered, somewhere in Putney," recorded Murry in his autobiography, *Between Two Worlds*, "a cyclist battalion of the Middlesex Regiment that was enlisting men. Why should I not go too? And Kingsmill's cheerful holiday face, combined with the cycles, seemed to put a more human complexion on the event." And so he went. But on returning from Putney he recalled that for some time he had been "counting on a holiday in Cornwall," and regretting his earlier decision to enlist, or, as his biographer Mr. F. A. Lea puts it, "having come to his senses" he quickly obtained a medical certificate to the effect that he had recently had pleurisy and might develop consumption and posted it to Putney before hurrying down himself to Cornwall.

After the war he and Kingsmill occasionally met and seem to have got on quite well. At one of their meetings Murry said that during the first year of the war he had gone about with the constant expectation of a heavy hand descending upon his shoulder, and a sergeant-major's voice announcing that he was under arrest.

As disciples of Frank Harris, they both met under difficult circumstances. Murry was temperamentally less suited than Kingsmill to Frank Harris's way of life, but he was by no means the only admirer who, in his very first attempt to live up to Harris's ideals, had contracted gonorrhoea. Kingsmill's exuberant manner may well have seemed overwhelming to Murry. Malcolm Muggeridge noticed that he had this effect on a number of people. "People were liable to shy away from him like frightened horses . . . because he made . . . [them] suddenly doubtful about themselves and the importance of their activities. He blew like a fresh wind into places where the dust had settled, stirring it up and making those who were there cough and splutter a little. His influence was too strong to be generally palatable."

This exuberance became more mellowed with the years, but

even when they met in 1911, Kingsmill struck the more
fastidious and diffident Murry as "a cheerful, hilarious, breezy
and altogether disarming fellow, whom I couldn't help liking."
Murry seems to have been favourably disposed towards
Kingsmill's *D. H. Lawrence.* The underlying theme of this
book, the will versus the imagination, is present in various
forms in nearly all his other books. In *Matthew Arnold* the
imagination was represented by Arnold's poetic temperament,
in conflict against his father's stronger influence of the will. In
The Return of William Shakespeare the theme is again present
in Shakespeare's desire for power mixing uneasily with his longing for love and an ideal harmony. In *Blondel*, all the characters whose desire is undivided come to a catastrophic end. In
the case of D. H. Lawrence, the clash took place between
Lawrence's mother, who embodied the will, and "Miriam"
who tried to release what was spiritual in Lawrence's nature.
In one of the first passages in his book, Kingsmill illuminates
the significance of this struggle.

"During the ten years with Miriam, Lawrence was
fighting to integrate his nature, so that he might be able
to develop the genius which he felt he possessed. But his
mother's will, imposed on him before he was born,
proved too strong for the imaginative and spiritual element
to which Miriam appealed, as it had previously proved
too strong for the tenderness he inherited from his father.
The spell which his mother exercised over him was not
the physical one he pretended to Miriam when he said he
had loved his mother like a lover. That was an attempt to
lay his doubts about his claim to be 'grand animal.' His
subjection to his mother was less melodramatic and far
deeper. He needed her to protect him against the fear
which overwhelmed him when he rose above the will into
the imagination. She had wrapped him round in her will,
and Miriam took the wrappings off, and so his need of
Miriam was always followed by a recoil of fear."

18

Novelist and Poet

FOR A NUMBER OF YEARS KINGSMILL HAD BEEN WORKING ON A
novel, but was dissatisfied with his original two drafts, the first
under the title *The Flying Dutchman*, the second called *The
Shore*. The final idea of how to set and climax the work came
to him after Brian, his younger brother, had fallen off the top
of a bus one morning in March 1939, and was taken to hospital with a cracked skull. When Kingsmill arrived at the
hospital he found Brian in bed unconscious, looking very impressive, and "breathing heavily with a stern look on his face,
as though the rest of us had been tried and found wanting." It
occurred to him later that such a fall might liberate and eluci-
date the mystical significance of life. Shortly after this, when
Arnold, the eldest brother, entered the ward, Kingsmill hurried
across to him, leaving the motionless figure of Brian on his bed,
in his eagerness to explain this new idea for his novel. Arnold's
reply was not encouraging. "Brian has fallen on his head," he
said, "not on your feet."

The Fall appeared in 1940, and being well received by the
critics at the time is generally regarded now as Kingsmill's most
satisfactory novel. Edwin Muir considered it to be one of the
finest novels in the decade, while as accomplished and professional a novelist as Graham Greene also thought very highly of
it, and a few faint echoes of it can perhaps be detected in his
own *The Heart of the Matter*. No contrivance is used in *The
Fall* as in Kingsmill's other novels to dissociate himself from
the central character in the book so as to achieve some degree
of impartiality and detachment, the result being that this central figure, an impecunious middle-aged author named William

Barr, is completely identified with Kingsmill himself. Although the context is not strictly autobiographical, many of the episodes narrated are taken more or less directly from Kingsmill's life, and William Barr's background and life before the novel commences, which is several times alluded to, is almost identical to his own.

The novel itself is divided into three separate parts. The first part opens in January 1939 with William's wife Rose, from whom he has been separated for nearly twelve years, asking him for a divorce, and it continues with a picture of William's life at this time—isolated, often depressed and lonely. The gloom is further intensified by the threat of war hanging over the country, which mirrors William's personal dejection if it does not amplify it, and thickens the seldom relieved melancholy of these pages.

The second part switches the narrative back in time to the late summer of 1926 to deal with William's unsatisfactory marriage and to describe a love-affair which he had in Switzerland with a young girl called Ruth—an obvious account of Kingsmill's own love-affair in that country which had led to his divorce and his leaving the family business.

In the third and final part, which follows directly on in time from the first part, William falls off a bus and, taken to hospital, has a vision in which he is given a momentary glimpse into the mystery of life. The book ends, after a discussion with a friend on personal immortality, with William furnishing the evidence necessary for his wife's divorce.

The novel as a whole is noteworthy for its fine incisive writing and austere presentation. Such similes and metaphors as he employs are usually of a kind that do not reduce but expand and illuminate the image, and invoke a sense of beauty and sometimes of wonder which lend ordinary events an added dimension, transmuting them into poetry. Kingsmill, was usually impatient of and uninterested in what he considered to be the everyday wearisome trivialities of this life, so that when they are touched upon, as at times was inevitable, the treatment is sketchy, commonplace and unrevealing. His fiction in general presents a curious anomaly, being compact yet at the same time discursive, and forming altogether an unsatisfactory compound of lyrical compression and diffuse superfluity. His prose throughout *The Fall* is clear and simple and contains several passages of exquisite beauty. But the very clarity of this style often accentuates the sentimentality of his feelings. Unlike another contemporary novelist, Henry Green, he could never resort to concentrated stylistic techniques into which he could drain his excess of sentiment and yearning, giving the writing a romantic flavour while leaving a hard core of reality. But on the other hand he avoided the pitfalls of such methods, for his humour is never facetious, his lyricism never pretentious. His inventive plot, though, was never so strong, as in the case for example of Patrick Hamilton's novels, to command a steady detachment. Behind the subtle irony of his prose there lurks some sense of insecurity; beneath the classical cadence, the distinctive closely-wrought precision and impartial restraint runs the undercurrent of a passionate and romantic imagination.

As in his life of Johnson, he permits himself no deviation from the central theme, no unnecessary or irrelevant padding, and the tone throughout is sensitive and tender. But the book makes harrowing reading and its general effect on the reader is to depress him. The dialogue, too, is compressed, sometimes to the point of parody, as he recounts with weary dispassion the continuous threats, pleas and bickerings of Rose, who is his first wife, Eileen.

The theme which lies behind this account of the Barrs' marital incompatibility is similar again to that in his *D. H. Lawrence,* being the clash between the will, symbolized by Rose's desire to dominate all of her husband's life, and the imagination, embodied by William's passionate longing for serenity and happiness at whatever cost. Rose, terrified by life, turns to William for safety and for refuge from fear, but so possessive is she that she cannot abide the thought of him carrying on any existence independent of her own, either in the company of his "clever friends" or even after she has died, going so far as to make him promise to kill himself should she die first. William's own imagination is undermined by his weakness, for he dismisses the possibility of being firm with Rose as "not practical politics," by which he can only mean that he had not the courage to be quite ruthless with someone he once loved. Sentimentalists are often spontaneously ruthless but seldom ruthless by premeditation and William, who possesses little or no will-power, in seeking for a short cut to happiness only succeeds in remaining in a prolonged hell.

As in nearly all his fiction the impression which emerges most vividly is the intensity of Kingsmill's own longing—"As soon as he was alone, everything but Ruth vanished from his consciousness, and he broke down, overwhelmed by the uprush of his longing for a happiness which for many years he had ceased to believe attainable in life." From his mesmerized wonder in the company of Ruth, it is easy to see how he came to marry a girl so temperamentally unsuited to him as Rose. The chapter which describes their love while they are together for a few days in Switzerland is suffused with a haunting quality produced by a mingling of tenderness, beauty, and an agony of longing behind which hovers a dark cloud of apprehension. The insuperable obstacles in the way of their love, the fleeting yet timeless nature of its progress, all add to the illusion of its potential perfection, for "the half was greater than the whole in love as well as art. It was those inconclusive experiences one remembered most vividly."

Neither Rose nor Ruth are presented except through the eyes of William, so that his marital trials are exaggerated and oversimplified at times, while Ruth's renunciation of him, not through her reverence for the institution of marriage which would be bad enough, but, as he sees it, through the preferment of her guardian's money to his own impoverished affection, does not ring true to what little we know of Ruth. At the close, we are left with the impression that William is harbouring a mistakenly embittered grievance against the nature of things. The girl on whom Ruth is based and who, during their few short days together in Switzerland, called forth Kingsmill's deepest emotions of love, had, it is true, left him in favour of her guardian's money. But this, rather than exonerating Kingsmill's treatment of Ruth in *The Fall*, spotlights the weakness and irresolution of his technique. In biography or autobiography one is bound by fact; in fiction one may be guided by it. Throughout the novel, Kingsmill steered a course very close to fact, and in some places, such as where Ruth rejects William, the last vestiges of his precarious objectivity crumble away under the pressure of his personal feelings, and he switches with abrupt and startling incongruity from fiction to pure autobiography.

Even in the last part of *The Fall*, where William, lying in hospital, sees his vision into the mystery of life, neither Rose nor Ruth are seen impartially, and in this lack of detachment lies the failure of the book. In the first part both vitality and redeeming humour are lacking; in the second, pathos is absent; in the third, William's heightened visionary insight is something of an anti-climax, it being still largely subjective.

Ignorance, or the lack of something creates illusion in the human mind. The inconclusive nature of his love affair, followed by Ruth's renunciation of him, deprived William of the hope, so suddenly rekindled within him from the days of his childhood, of a lasting happiness in this life, but fostered the illusion that such perfect ecstasy had been momentarily within his grasp only to be snatched cruelly away from him. "Suddenly he saw her face, indistinct in the darkness, and her fair hair flowing over her white nightdress and then she was gone." Back in the nightmare of his everyday existence, as his expectation of personal felicity on earth peters out, so nourishment is automatically provided for the second illusion of a happiness waiting for him somewhere else. He could not be cheated for ever of the ecstasy he felt was buried somewhere within him.

Kingsmill's intuitional optimism was like a great river in flood, which stopped in its course by practical experience, rose and reached out over unknown territory, beyond the limits of its banks. His religious beliefs, however, were not merely a reaction from his worldly disappointments. Formed early in life, they were based on thought, which told him that life on earth treated as a complete and self-contained experience did not make sense; on intuition, which suggested to him that there was a divine element in the nature of mankind; and on personal emotions, in which one might perhaps savour some foretaste of a timeless ecstasy. The normal sights of this world, of nature, he treated as symbols of some other life, and behind the ordinary events of everyday existence he saw the workings of an extraordinary and ineffable power. "The world is real, houses and trees, men and women, motor buses and the moaning sea, but we have all fallen asleep, and these things, these simple and reasonable things, have been confused for us."

Nowhere is his own peculiar blending of melancholy and mystical optimism more clearly and, in places, beautifully expressed than in his poem, *Night and Morning*. This poem, was begun at about the same time as *The Fall* and belongs to this period, having arisen out of the same visional inspiration as that novel. It opens on a clear moonlit night with the poet reflecting on the duration of man's tribulation on earth:

"How long, how long, till the last moon shall wane,
    And the night cover man's accomplished pain?"

He sleeps and the night flows on, the moon sinks out of sight and, shortly before the dawn, "in the empty hour before the light, when there is only nothingness and night," he wakes again and gazes out across the world.

"The blank night stretched before him, everywhere
    Man shut within his loneliness and fear,
    Each soul a point of solitary pain,
    On, on to where, another day began,
    Earth turned her waters to the burning sun
    And from the night's oblivion and dismay,
    Man rose to the vain labour of the day."

The mood and emotion of these lines bears a resemblance to some of the *Last Poems* of A. E. Housman whom Kingsmill once described as a "diminutive Johnson," and they admirably reveal the more melancholic earthbound side of his nature which overwhelmed him when his faith and vitality weakened, his eyes lost sight of eternity and he became immersed in the troubled waters of time.

The dawn then breaks and the dolorous veil is dissolved before the poet's eyes. A breath of expectancy fills him, rising high into his lungs, and he feels the falling away of those two earthly tormentors, hope and fear.

> "And no more need to hope nor cause for fear,
> No wounds received or given any more,
> And on the pebbles of the brightening shore,
> Beside the murmur that the ripples made,
> The mystery asleep, the burden laid."

After this revelation, an upsurge of lightness and release flood through him, and falling asleep once more he dreams that he is back again in his beloved Switzerland. In this visionary dream, the picture of spring, bright with blossom, is evoked with a heightened poetic illumination and a subtle and imaginative simplification. No detail in the pattern seems omitted, everything has the appearance of falling inevitably into its rightful place in the scheme of things, and the whole picture snaps into dazzling focus. With this scene the poems ends.

> "The bright air quivered on a dome of snow,
> And spring was blossoming on the plains below,
> And every murmur to the horizon's bound
> Was echoed in the water's gentle sound,
> And even the grains of sand shone like the sun,
> And near and far and everywhere was one."

Much of the elegance and distinction of the whole poem can be judged from the lines quoted, as can its weaknesses

which consist of a slight vagueness in his moulding of the outside shell of the poem and a lack of absolutely concise, expanding and enlarging imagery at its core. The accent in some of
the lines accentuates what is inessential and conveys a sense
of rhythmic mechanical flatness. Initially Kingsmill wrote two
poems and these he later assimilated into the longer *Night and
Morning.* As in many instances where a final version is much
fuller and longer than the original, the first vibrant and pulsing
essence is diluted with matter released only by secondary inspiration, the primary force and intensity weakened with after-
thoughts.

19

Schoolmaster and Editor

KINGSMILL INTERRUPTED HIS RE-WRITING OF *The Fall* AT THE end of April 1939, when he sailed with his mother to Cork on a visit to her sister. Although he had loved Ireland when young, this journey was more in the nature of duty than a holiday and, involving delay to his novel, gave rise to feelings of despondency as the ship drew near the Irish coast. "From the moment I saw its sad fields and straggling trees from the deck of the ship," he wrote, "I felt depressed. Nothing seemed solid. As we steamed up to the docks, Cork looked unreal, as though the genuine Cork was being held in reserve, and this shabby imitation had been dumped down overnight. The melancholia in the eyes of the men hanging round the docks was like something seen in a dream."

His spirits were not heightened by an episode which took place the next day. Deciding to revisit the place where his grandfather had lived he set out late that morning. Walking through the town, which seemed to have retained all the decay but little of the liveliness he remembered from his early years, he passed the rectory and continued up towards Hillside, a house set high above the surrounding country, where used to live a girl with whom he had once fallen deeply in love while a boy on holiday with his grandparents. "A distant view of the sea," he wrote, "and the beauty of the landscape and the blissful pain of adoring the unresponsive Cecily formed a whole which I had never altogether forgotten."

But as he approached the house an undercurrent of unusually strong misgiving weakened the anticipated pleasure of indulging his feelings of nostalgia. And not without reason. Cecily and her mother had prudently retreated to England many years back, after her sister, Gwendolen, had married the son of the local washerwoman and then given birth to a number of children, one of whom had set fire—accidentally it was rumoured—to the house which had been almost entirely consumed and now stood a charred and burnt-out shell.

Repressing an impulse to turn back Kingsmill went up and knocked at a door. There was a shuffling within and the door was opened to reveal Gwendolen, no longer the strikingly attractive young girl he remembered, but withered and toothless, her cheeks rough and coarse, her hair dusty, her clothes tattered and untidy. She recognized him at once, ushered him in and setting him down before a glass of lime juice began to talk about the past. At first she spoke quite coherently of the times they had spent together in Switzerland, but soon she grew increasingly restless and disconnected as she passed to the subject of her late husband's prowess as a lover. By the time she had reached the present she was completely incoherent, claiming to have developed powers which had been largely responsible for the settlement at Munich, and to possess the trick of foretelling certain financial changes in the international scene by studying cloud formation.

He returned thankfully to England shortly before his birthday to recommence work on the novel. He was by now fifty years of age. Stocky, his figure built more for comfort than speed, and slightly below average height like most of the heros of his novels, with a high, noble forehead and fastidious, well-shaped nose, his face was one of extraordinary sensitivity. "And also it was a jovial face," records William Gerhardi, "and also austere when in thought, with his greying hair raised in the wind." His eyes still glinted with vitality and fun, but his expression was mostly of sorrow and the pain of life. The same contrast can be seen in the death mask taken ten years later. The front view shows a fine face suffused with warmth and humour and topped with a magnificent, dome-like forehead.

The two profiles are of an old, care-worn man, whose downward sloping lines are taut with strain and worry.

In the same year as the publication of *The Fall,* Kingsmill wrote :

> "In an age of private and public earthquakes I have frequently had to move farther and faster than suited my temperament. This has doubtless been good for me and my work, but I should be glad if my last years could be passed in the tranquillity suitable to my nature, and in adding to the number of my novels—for in spite of the great interest biography has for me, I do not think it possible to go as deep in biography as in fiction."

But it was not to be. In May 1940, the shortage of teaching staff led to him becoming a schoolmaster at Marlborough, while his family moved down to Somerset. At first he was lonely, but he soon got to like the masters even though he found the restraint of being unable to throw off his shoes and put up his feet in their presence at times rather wearisome. The boys, too, he found delightful, though some of them were stupid enough. On one occasion, while he was reading Johnson's life of Swift to them, he paused to ask what meaning they attached to "Swift had one of those minds which astonish the world with their early pregnancy." Vexed by the idiot dumbness which greeted this question, he asked "Do you think it means that Swift took a long time about becoming a mother?" "I will not say they jumped at this solution," he told a friend later, "but several of them brightened perceptibly."

The first few weeks of teaching exhausted him, but he soon arrived at a method of passing the working hours to the equal satisfaction of himself and the form. His practice was to read out the précis of a story, such as Maupassant's *Necklace,* and then get the boys to write down what they could remember of it. "This précis," he told another of the masters who inquired how he was managing, "I propose to read out to the second class also. To the third class of the day I shall read from the proofs of my *Johnson without Boswell*. The fourth class, by a gentleman's agreement, will read, like gentlemen, in the privacy of their own studies or elsewhere, or not at all. To my fifth and last class I propose to read a précis of Maupassant's *Necklace*."

After two terms he left Marlborough and took a position at the Merchant Taylors school in Middlesex where he varied his teaching technique to the extent of substituting Eckermann's *Conversations with Goethe* for Johnson's *Lives of the Poets*. He remained here for four terms before being appointed literary editor of *Punch* in 1942.

He did not enjoy the routine of office life and always appeared to be only a casual observer in the *Punch* offices. Nor did he hurry unduly when the bombs began to fall, and would "wander about the streets," Hesketh Pearson records, "hatless as usual, and chat with the air-raid wardens as if nothing more remarkable was in progress than a display of fireworks on Guy Fawkes night."

Malcolm Muggeridge has given a vivid picture of what he must have looked like about this time, "making his way along the Strand with that rolling gait of his, books under his arm, and looking round with a kind of wonder and slight comical bewilderment very characteristic of him, and then, when he saw a familiar face, his eye lighting up—'Hallo, old man, hallo!'"

His appearance on these occasions was completed by an old brief-case, usually empty, which he carried about with him wherever he went and which he called his "Sedley", a name originally given to it in 1927 by his brother Brian, because Kingsmill's affectionate attachment to it reminded him of Thackeray's Mr. Sedley, who also had a case for his papers after he had left his business.

As a member of the *Punch* staff during the war, he was sometimes required to do fire duty in the offices at night. The procedure for this appears to have been quite simple and ought not to have provided scope for personal eccentricity. "Our system (an excellent one)" he explained, "is not to get out of bed unless blown out by a direct hit, and even then it's left to one's own judgment. The windows are blacked out with a wooden frame which deadens all sound, so all one hears is a faint popping as of corks."

Despite the congenial element of passivity at the root of this scheme, Kingsmill succeeded in differentiating between his own hours of duty and those of his colleagues. Wandering about from room to room, and up and down the various passages, he would knock over so many ink stands, papers and books, and dislodge with the impact of a knee or a shoulder so many fixtures, as the word is, that the staff, returning to work the following morning could never be certain as to whether or not there had been a bomb explosion the previous night.

Kingsmill was sometimes self-conscious about his clumsiness. Of other minor eccentricities he seems, for the most part to have been vaguely unaware. He always dressed quite normally but had no great interest in clothes and would put on the first jacket or coat to hand, usually the one he had worn the previous day until, to his surprise, its delapidated and threadbare appearance would occasion comment among his friends.

Like many absent-minded people he was aware that his friends considered him vague and impractical without being able to reconcile himself fully to their unanimous opinion. The awkwardness which his brother-officers had noticed and re-marked upon while in the army clung to him for the rest of his life. But even when, on one occasion, he had inadvertently sat on some of William Gerhardi's gramophone records, he appealed later the same afternoon to Hesketh Pearson, "I'm not really clumsy, am I?" resting one of his feet on the marble side of the mantelpiece which instantly came away from the wall as he finished speaking, and fell with a loud crash to the floor.

Such episodes as this, or the displacing, on another occasion of a firegrate with the consequential distribution of several live coals over the carpet, were always greeted with shouts of laughter by Kingsmill himself, sometimes to the added dismay of the owner of the broken or damaged article in question. He would seldom tender an apology either, for damage caused, preferring instead to raise his unwieldiness to the level of impersonal generalization so that its particular occasion was submerged in a universal acceptance of the inherent imperfection of life. William Gerhardi had another way of looking at such incidents : "Hugh Kingsmill," he wrote, "usually broke something or set something on fire in mere inadvertency, and when I proffered the mildest objection would exclaim in the voice of a man outraged in his deepest feelings, "Damn it all, you're the host!' identifying the vocation of a host with that of a martyr."

The sensitiveness which went along with this lumbering awkwardness is equally striking. Hesketh Pearson indeed attributes Kingsmill's reluctance to look anyone in the face while speaking to him as directly due to this extreme and over-acute sensitivity. At cocktail parties, too, he would manoeuvre himself surreptitiously into some corner of the room and talk only to his personal friends unless constantly reminded of his social duty.

With many people he was quick to take offence. In 1943 Llewelyn Powys's correspondence was published, edited by one of Kingsmill's friends, Louis Wilkinson. In one of Powys's letters there appeared a reference to "a Hugh Lunn man-of-the-world tone"—which Kingsmill, much to Louis Wilkinson's astonishment, considered malicious. After reading it he wrote a letter to Wilkinson in which he implied that his personal enemies, annoyed by his persistent unworldliness, would be evilly delighted with the worldly tone attributed to him. This fantastic and far-fetched notion reveals the sense of persecution which simmered below the surface of his nature, and which on occasions boiled over in the course of his life. Most frequently this side of him showed itself in his guarded, almost suspicious manner which was well described by one of his friends as a "mistrustful touchiness." But sometimes it developed more strongly into something not far removed from paranoia. As might be expected, the most extreme example of this tendency is to be found during the months following his withdrawal from the family business, at one point in which he bitterly remarked, "How I hate this solitude. Is it not typical of life that I who love my fellow-creatures should be segregated, while a lot of callous, cold-blooded swine are comfortably domiciled."

As in the case of most people prone to sentimentality he could be morbidly touchy, and this mood usually overcame him after the commercial failure of his last book on which, during the previous months, he had pinned such unrealistically high hopes. But the question of money in general always inflamed his sense of unrelieved persecution. Despite their frequent protestations to the contrary, he continued to regard many of his friends as rich men—a logical preconception to the request for a loan. One such victim was Louis Wilkinson who, under the pseudonym of "Louis Marlow" had written a number of novels and other books. When he reacted to this unfair and inaccurate surmise of personal affluence by speaking jokingly about "the Marlow millions" Kingsmill elected to take him seriously. On the other hand he could prove both unselfish and sympathetic towards those who finally succeeded in convincing him that their circumstances were no brighter than his own. Graham Greene, on one occasion, remarked that if he were a poor man, he felt that he would always be able to rely on Kingsmill for assistance.

Everything with Kingsmill was a personal matter, and he was always conscious of other people's ungenerous lack of sympathy. In particular he reacted quickly to hostile or unappreciative reviews, and it was due to a mixture of pride and sensitivity that whereas he despised bad adverse criticism he could never endure it. This inability could lead to unfortunate results and was partially responsible for his failure to achieve some more extravagant distinction in the literary world.

From 1927 until the end of his life he contributed numerous articles and reviews to socialist, independent and conservative periodicals, without identifying himself with their politics, and was consequently regarded by the proprietors and editors concerned as somewhat unpredictable. During the 1940's, he wrote in *The New English Review* a form of testimony to his political beliefs. "I do not wish to pretend that I am editing a literary supplement on a Tory review by pure chance," he explained, "or that my sympathies are equally divided between Right and Left. On the Right there is room for those who believe that the individual is the only absolute unit, and that all larger units are temporal and transient groupings." But though Kingsmill was deeply concerned with the individual, he had no real knowledge or interest whatever in politics, and felt that it had little place in literature. Once, during the time of the Spanish Civil War, he met one of its literary and intellectual enthusiasts in the Strand who announced excitedly that he was shortly off to Spain. Kingsmill, who was thinking about something else, replied absent-mindedly : "I suppose the cost of living is cheap out there."

By the same token it was for no political reason that he was writing for *The New English Review*, but because his friend Douglas Jerrold was editor and had the foresight to allow him a comparatively free hand in the literary supplement. The relationship between Kingsmill and Jerrold though was by no means free from friction and when someone once accused him of possessing an anti-Jerrold complex, he replied, "An anti-Jerrold simplex you mean; there's nothing complex about disliking Jerrold." Yet it was Douglas Jerrold's leniency and imagination which made possible Kingsmill's finest literary essays, one of which, on Sir Walter Scott, began :

"Having spent a good deal of February reading Sir Walter Scott after an attack of influenza, I am sorry that no one has written of him of late, for duty and inclination would both have been complied with had I been able to connect the following reflections with some study of Scott just issuing from the press."

Although he took a great deal of trouble over all his essays, inclination rather than strict duty was usually in the ascendant in those which he wrote for *The New English Review* and which were later published in *The Progress of a Biographer,* the publisher's note of which states that Kingsmill belonged to no body, secular or religious.

Most of the periodicals for which he wrote were prepared to let him continue contributing so long as he did not offend the general policy any too blatantly. Kingsmill himself was less accommodating; he resented the slightest interference with his work and his response to any editorial objections was similar to that of Pontius Pilate to the chief priests: "What I have written I have written."

Differences of opinion were bound to spring up under such conditions, and his retirement from *Time and Tide*, for which he wrote book reviews for several months, illustrates the way in which he was dictated to by feelings which all writers possess but most manage to subdue when it becomes a matter of writing something to be printed or nothing at all. In July 1935, under the title "This Ever-Diverse Pair" he reviewed Walter Dexter's edition of Dickens's letters to his wife, in the course of which he asserted that Dickens had never been in love with Catherine Hogarth as she believed him to have been, not even during their engagement. "Fresh from the capriciousness of Maria Beadnell," he wrote, ". . . he [Dickens] had become engaged on the rebound . . . [and] had no feelings stronger than any pretty girl inspires in an ardent young man."

The week after this review appeared Bernard Shaw protested against this view in a long letter which, for advertisement purposes, was made into a leading article by *Time and Tide*. After stating that Dickens may well have driven his wife crazy by the too rapid exploitation of her fertility, that Dickens and she were totally unsuited to each other when the babies eventually ceased, and Dickens was frequently convulsed with merriment by his wife's comic aspects at the table, Shaw concluded, "Mrs. Dickens was right: Charles did love her a great deal more ardently than was good for either of them, and so her point is carried and the incident closed."

But, as may well be imagined, the incident was far from closed where Kingsmill was concerned. He cared for Shaw, on the whole, little better than for Dickens, considering him to be under-sexed and over successful, and was not slow in sending back his reply. "To be championed in the lists of love by George Bernard Shaw," he wrote, "is exactly the kind of misfortune which Mrs. Dickens, unluckiest of women, would attract." And he went on to remind Shaw that in the preface to *Getting Married* he had spoken of "the unnaturally sustained concupiscences" of marriage, and left him to reconcile this phrase with his theory that Dickens, who never troubled to conceal his disgust at his wife's pregnancies, was in love with her.

This letter was refused by the assistant editress of *Time and Tide* under the plea that the office was stacked with letters from people anxious to associate their names in print with that of Shaw, and that were they all to be published a separate edition of the paper would be needed. "We get so many letters," she wrote, "which specialize in being offensive to him [Shaw] that we have to make it a rule not to publish them."

Kingsmill was furious and immediately went round to the offices of *Time and Tide* in person to point out that since Shaw's letter was a direct and challenging answer to his own article, he was surely in a somewhat different position from these other correspondents. Not to make any reply, he added unrealistically, might affect not only his literary status but also the sales of his future books. It was then suggested that he rephrase his letter less vigorously, but he declined this suggestion, having no desire "to keep on rewriting my letter until it harmonized with the editorial policy of protecting Mr. Shaw's dignity from the results of his imprudence."

Though his sentiments were doubtless intellectually superior, his unwise and hot-headed action amounted almost to irresponsibility, with its obvious cut in earnings for him at a time when, according to himself, money was extremely short, the only people to suffer as the outcome of the whole episode being the Kingsmill family itself. "In their financial aspect," he once wrote, "the lives of most writers, painters and musicians suggest a man leaping from ice floe to ice floe across a wide and rapid river. A strenuous, not a dignified spectacle." In Kingsmill's case, the sensitivity produced by the unsuitable and at times hostile background to his early years, when he always felt himself to be undervalued and unappreciated by his family, reinforced his natural impracticability. "For Hughie, alas," wrote Malcolm Muggeridge, "the distance between the ice-floes did not grow any less with the years, and the jumping from one to the other made him increasingly breathless."

It was only to be expected under these circumstances that he would feel tempted himself to undervalue anyone who rose to succeed where he had failed. He felt impatience with a writer such as Desmond MacCarthy, who employed, he thought, a subtlety of mind almost equal to his own in paying his contemporaries a series of appropriate compliments, remotely qualified. But in envying such another writer's moderate popularity he overestimated its effect which, in MacCarthy's case at least, did little to dispense the rueful sense of disappointment he felt in the extent of his literary achievement. Both Kingsmill and MacCarthy were delightful company and both believed in meeting personally as many people as possible in their early years who might conceivably assist them in their literary careers. But Kingsmill was not one of those men, to use Lance Sieveking's somewhat rueful words, whose critical faculty was in abeyance when reading the work of a friend or acquaintance, whatever elevated literary position he held. Consequently MacCarthy, with his charming and eloquent fusing of flattery and honesty rose to become, by common consent, the foremost literary critic in journalism of his day—"the best of contemporary critics," as Raymond Mortimer called him—while Kingsmill, esteemed more as a conversationalist and wit than as a writer, found his creative work ignored. His bewilderment at this neglect is excessive, for he often wounded other people's feelings by what he wrote. For example, in reviewing *Ego 5* by James Agate, he wrote : "Everyone, it is said, has one good book inside him and, if this be so, it would be unkind to suggest that Mr. James Agate is the exception that proves the rule. All one can in fairness say is that his good book is not among the thirty-six he has so far produced." Agate promptly replied in *Ego 6* : "To justify this statement 'H.K.' must have read all thirty-six books. To continue in feverish search after thirty-five disappointments—here's tribute indeed." But Agate had been hurt by this review and took it in a less humorous manner than he lead his readers to believe. Meeting Hesketh Pearson some time later at the Savage Club he spoke of Kingsmill with extreme bitterness. Pearson replied that he was one of his greatest friends and a delightful person, but Agate continued to fulminate until Colin Hurry appeared and assured Agate that what Pearson was saying was no less than the truth. Agate then proceeded to quote Kingsmill's review of *Ego 5* and Colin Hurry replied encouragingly, "Oh, but Hughie won't bear you any malice for that!" upon which Agate jumped to his feet and disappeared in a rage from the club.

The same sensitivity which provoked him at times to react to situations with spontaneous passion also made him one of the most endearing of friends. Towards the close of his life Malcolm Muggeridge wrote to Hesketh Pearson that he felt if Kingsmill died half the pleasure of living would, at one stroke, be gone. He was one of the most sympathetic, humorous and genial of companions. Often his friends, intending to bid him farewell at the door of their home, would find themselves first walking along the street with him, then next to him on a bus and finally saying a regretful goodbye outside his own home an hour or so later. On the circle line of the underground, a number of his friends were so taken up with his company that they missed their station and went on to complete the full circuit. And on one notable occasion Brian Lunn, seeing his brother off one morning at Victoria station on his way to

France, found himself the same afternoon passportless and at loggerheads with the French authorities at Boulogne.

This affectionate and receptive quality which made his friends reluctant to part from him also attracted strangers, eager to impart the story of their lives to a sympathetic audience. "His very presence," wrote Hesketh Pearson, "invited confidence." There was a look of compassion and humanity in his face, his eyes, which reassured and consoled one. His affectionate nature together with his stimulating companionship persuaded most people to overlook any social inadequacy. Visiting Alan White during the war years when all food was severely rationed, he used up a week's supply of sugar in one short week-end, and when Dorothy, his wife, made some mild reprimand he replied with childlike simplicity that he liked sugar. But his presence more than made up for the ensuing week's sacrifice, and he always remained a welcome guest.

He was, again like a child, enormously fond of all sweet things from rich chocolate to creamy cakes. When his eldest daughter, Kathleen, was a child, and Kingsmill was supposed to be suffering from diabetes, he used to bribe her for chocolates which she sold to him for a franc each when he came upstairs to kiss her goodnight; and during the day he would induce her to let him have pieces of sugar *gratis*. Colin Hurry, the poet, also noticed that "he had the zest and curiosity of an adolescent schoolboy. He was very fond of cream buns and the sight of such delicacies would bring the same gleam to his eyes as would a conversational opening. This simplicity made him the idol of many children, for he never condescended to them. He was one of them."

Except perhaps in his last years, when much of his vitality had ebbed away, he was at his best with children, companionable, affectionate and understanding. And as they idolized him, he did not need to crave for something beyond his reach. He had nothing of the tyrant, and his own children's dependence on him was an altogether beneficial influence so far as he was concerned, for though they might intensify his financial worries, their presence brought out his tenderness and dispelled for a time that vibrant yearning which, repressed beneath his genial exterior, sometimes curdled into envy and erupted to the surface in sudden and unexpected bursts of irritability. With women his relationship was always aggravated by desire and with men he was always acutely conscious of his own comparative lack of recognition and financial success. When William Gerhardi mentioned the sum of money he was receiving as an advance for one of his books, Kingsmill stopped suddenly in his tracks and a green flush seemed to spread over his astonished features. "It's not envy, old man," he explained once he had recovered from the initial shock, "just longing."

20

"The Poisoned Crown"

DURING THE WAR YEARS KINGSMILL WAS ENGAGED ON WRITING another book over which he spent much time and which gave him a great amount of trouble. The completion of *The Poisoned Crown*, as it was called, was further delayed by his various jobs as a schoolmaster and literary editor, and it did not finally come out until 1944. It contained studies of Elizabeth, Cromwell, Napoleon and Lincoln, and was prefixed by a closely written chapter on "The Genealogy of Hitler." This chapter, one of the most brilliant that he ever wrote, set out to analyse and plot the course of modern romanticism and Utopianism by means of examining a series of representative poets and men of action from Rousseau to Hitler, by way of Napoleon, Byron, Victor Hugo, Heine, Balzac, Dostoievsky, Neitzsche, H. G. Wells, Charlie Chaplin and others.

It might seem strange that someone who stood so far apart from the *zeitgeist* of his own age should choose to scrutinize so often and with such knowledge and acuteness the *zeitgeist* of other ages. The explanation for this apparent paradox is to be found in the pleasure Kingsmill derived out of diminishing the proportions of such demi-gods by the detachment of his style and by the ultimate perfection against which he matched them. He liked to demonstrate that writers are idolized "not because they love their fellow-men, which is never a recommendation and in extreme instances leads to crucifixion, but because their self-love is in tune with current fears and desires, and in giving it expression they are speaking for an inarticulate multitude." Popularity and success, then, were usually the result of man's shortcomings rather than his virtues,

for such men "must necessarily be mediums of what is temporal, limited and egotistic in human nature rather than for
what aspires towards the universal life which underlies the
discord of time." The implication being that small sales and
continued neglect were the product of unflagging virtue and
undiminished endeavour, and carried with them the inevitable
reward of a greater and more spiritual nature, Kingsmill was
able to compensate himself for his own unrelieved obscurity in
the world of letters by exposing the great literary figures of the
past, Byron and Tennyson, Kipling and Dickens in the last
century. These men, he reflected not without some satisfaction,
who are hailed as geniuses during their lifetime, "are self-
absorbed much beyond the average, are prone to self-pity in
their youth and to misanthropy in their later years, and die
ringed round with glory but lonely and comfortless within."
Such were the consolations of worldly failure, such the pitfalls
and dangers which hounded the steps of those who succeeded
in capturing the glittering prize which Kingsmill always had in
view, but which, by this time, he must have realized, would
never come his way.

The intensity of his regret quickened Kingsmill's imagination
in the first chapter, the brilliance of which dims on first reading the remainder of the book. But the four chapters which
follow are models of short, concise biography. They are all
beautifully written and soundly constructed, and each one is
ventilated by his pungent and refreshing humour. The art of
compiling such studies lies, of course, in the intelligent selection of available data and the moulding together of such data
into a composite whole. This Kingsmill achieved with such
skill and apparent ease that his technique is quite unobtrusive.

As Kingsmill originally planned *The Poisoned Crown*, the
book was to include a study of Lenin, but Lenin got him down,
and at last he left him out altogether. By 1944 most people
were heartily sick of the idea of war and welcomed a treatise
which traced many of the thoughts underlying the conception
of dictatorship and which showed up the emptiness of the

illusory promise of power and the evil effects it wreaked on those who succumbed to its temptation. Most of the critics were impressed, and praised the book, sometimes a little erratically, but with general enthusiasm, and it was recommended by the Book Society—only the second of his works to be favoured in this manner. The final memorable paragraph of "The Genealogy of Hitler" is reproduced here in full, for apart from making clear the purpose of the volume, it gives some indication of the distinction of the writing and explains Kingsmill's own isolated position in the literary world.

"After a century and a half of emptying the divine out of life," he wrote, "the epoch which opened with the uniqueness and Utopianism of Rousseau has collapsed in the self-deification and the New Order of Hitler. Many remedies for a shattered world are now being offered to mankind, but they are all collective remedies, and collective remedies do not heal the ills produced by collective action. The purpose of this book is not to suggest the true remedy, except indirectly, but to illustrate the destructive effect of power. Naturally, it is not disputed that benefits of a secondary order may flow from the achievements of able rulers; it was clearly to the advantage of England in the second half of the sixteenth century to be governed by Queen Elizabeth and not by Queen Anne. But, on a much deeper level of reality, it was not to the advantage either of Elizabeth or of those who served her that she should set herself up as a semi-divine figure, a Virgin Queen exalted high above common humanity. What is divine in man is elusive and impalpable, and he is easily tempted to embody it in a concrete form—a church, a country, a social system, a leader—so that he may realize it with less effort and serve it with more profit. Yet, as even Lincoln proved, the attempt to externalize the Kingdom of Heaven in a temporal shape must end in disaster. It cannot be created by charters and constitutions

nor established by arms. Those who set out for it alone
will reach it together, and those who seek it in company
will perish by themselves."

While he was writing *The Poisoned Crown* and shortly
after he became literary editor of *Punch* he brought his family
up to London once more, and took a flat for them in Ladbroke
Grove where they stayed until early in 1946, at which time they
moved to Westbourne Terrace before, the following year leaving London to live at a cottage called Binesfield near Horsham
in Sussex. To Malcolm Muggeridge, who on hearing of his
appointment on the *Punch* staff had written to offer congratulations on the improvement of his affairs, he replied on
the back of a writ, implying that any such congratulations at
this stage were premature. And to one of his unfortunate
creditors he began a letter "Enclosed please fail to find three
cheques." Of another such creditor who had written to point
out that he was now entitled to a full settlement, he commented
to the effect that the man's position would be more enviable
if his claim were weaker and his own finances stronger.

But despite all this, and despite, too, his description of one
publisher's advance as "more of a retreat than an advance,"
he was probably receiving more money during these few years
than at any other time since he left his father's business. Apart
from his salary from *Punch* and the money he obtained from
books published, he also received a small advance for his autobiography. The task of writing about oneself which Chekov
once described as verbal torture, Kingsmill found no less
arduous. By the end of his life he had completed only a quarter
of it, and though he seems to have been pleased with what he
had written, the pitfalls of self-consciousness and a lack of
detachment against both of which he was always on his guard
made the work so laborious and the prospect of continuing it
so tedious that his initial enthusiasm weakened and his progress
gradually slowed to a halt.

The trials which were afflicting the population of London

during these war years struck him as being less arduous than the personal prospect of completing this autobiography. He went without a ration book for several months and did not appear to have undergone undue hardship, while of other shortages, such as petrol, he was totally unaware. While the bombs were flying all round, he would play over to himself the slow movements from various gramophone records—the Nimrod variation in Elgar's Enigma, the slow movement of Beethoven's violin, triple and Emperor concertos. The gentle sadness of these passages soothed him, though at the same time they may well have unnerved some of his neighbours on hearing their long mournful notes echoing between the loud thunder of exploding bombs. These and other slow movements appealed increasingly to him during the last ten years of his life and he was on many occasions drawn away from completing his books in favour of listening to such music. But his musical appreciation was suspect, and he liked best to read a book while listening to records. Not surprisingly he disliked much of Wagner, and in his critical essay *The Comforts of Richard Wagner* he quoted with approval Amiel's view of *Tannhäuser,* that "it is music depersonalized—neo-Hegelian music—music multiple instead of individual. . . . This music has its root and its fulcrum in the tendencies of the epoch—materialism and socialism— each of them ignoring the true value of the human personality, and drowning it in the totality of Nature or of Society."

Although by no means averse to lighter, gayer music in its place—he enjoyed Gilbert and Sullivan—it is characteristic of him that he objected to its presence within serious compositions. Although he loved Beethoven's last quartet, he disapproved of the last movement where, after the agonizing question and the answer, sad and firm—*Muss es sein? Es muss sein*— everything is "thrown away" in a deliberate, buoyant and fantastic valediction—then let it be! This mood, which is reproduced in literature by such writers as Shakespeare and Chekov, usually displeased Kingsmill, and was, perhaps, the token of an element of caution which sprang up within him as a natural counterpart to the occasional spasms of emotional recklessness which, even in his early fifties, threatened at times to engulf him.

The mirage of that earthly happiness, which reason knew to be false, could still clutch at his heart, so that again and again as life went on he saw it afresh. Surrounded by his disenchanted contemporaries he would pass and repass each day a thousand unillumined faces, and still the mirage beckoned him on. Even now, when he seemed to have finally objectified the past, he could still not adapt himself to the present, or reconcile himself entirely to the future, for he could never strike what all the young at heart abhor, a compromise. And so he would watch himself carefully, knowing that his peace of mind, as always, might suddenly be destroyed in a moment by the flickering reappearance of that long-awaited promise of felicity, of release into happiness.

21

Apotheosis

WITH THE END OF THE WAR THE STAFF RETURNED TO *Punch* and Kingsmill became redundant. He gave up the literary editorship at the end of 1944, though continuing for several years to do short reviews for it, and in 1945 he became the literary editor of *The New English Review*, which seems all at once to have become staffed with many of the people who in past years had found themselves employed by the Lunn Travel Agency. Apart from his contributions to *Punch* and *The New English Review* during the last five years of his life, he produced his third talk and travel book, *Talking of Dick Whittington* in 1947, and in 1948 started on a new novel, *Miserimus.* Besides this he was also engaged in compiling his last completed anthology, *The High Hill of the Muses* which was published posthumously in 1955, and *The Genius of Carlyle* which was still unfinished at the time of his death.

His most important work during these last years was his critical essays for *The New English Review*. If some of his fiction lays bare what was weakest and most romantic in his nature, most of his biography and especially his literary criticism displays his finest and strongest qualities. When dealing with other people's lives he could step back and approach his subject from an unexpected direction, often with startlingly original and illuminating results. *The Progress of a Biographer*, his last book, being a collection of the literary criticisms he had written since the end of 1944, was published shortly before his death, and, containing his finest achievement in imaginative literature, attracted but little attention. As in the case of Johnson, if he had not been distinguished by the distributors of literary honours, he had "seldom descended to the arts by which favour is obtained." "Individuality," wrote Hesketh Pearson, "gains no credit on earth, until time has softened its peculiarity or brought it prestige. Hughie did not live long enough to lose the animosity of his inferiors."

Like most great literature the essays in *The Progress of a Biographer* rise to an impersonal significance, while being rooted in deep personal experience and recollected in tranquillity after a lifetime of struggling for recognition, after many years of unrelieved poverty and periods of intense emotional upheaval. It is difficult to know what to write of such a book; after all, there is the book itself, and if the reader is unable to detect first-hand the astonishing power of imagination which runs through it from the first page to the last, then little or nothing that anyone else can write will be of great assistance to him.

Those who knew Kingsmill personally and therefore read this book with some attention appreciated its outstanding quality instantly. Douglas Jerrold, the editor of *The New English Review Magazine*, and a personal friend of Kingsmill's for many years, wrote of him as a critic in the following words:

"He had two indispensable qualities—courage and detachment . . . [and] a vigorous assertion of critical standards. Kingsmill insisted first and foremost on the writer's need for integrated personality. A man's values must only be influenced by his good or ill-fortune, his prejudices or his sentiments in so far as these influences have been informed by reason, illuminated by imagination and disciplined by an act of will directed to the right end, the search for truth that is in men, the truth not that men speak but that men live. . . .

"It is characteristic of our times that Kingsmill's criticism, which is in fact classical in its approach, was regarded as idiosyncratic precisely because he was not seduced by what Conrad called 'the occasional utterance of elevated sentiments' by an author into attributing a quality of elevation to his work. . . . The creative artist must himself experience what he portrays. . . .

"The great body of his critical work will live, as surely as Johnson's *Lives of the Poets* have lived. It is so exact and . . . so direct . . . Kingsmill would, regardless of personal circumstances, spend days on a short article which, when finished, seemed so effortless, so 'necessary' in its conclusive logic, that the reader might and often did assume that it had been written in an hour or so."

But accurate and penetrating as this summary is, it can give little impression of the dazzling powers of insight displayed in *The Progress of a Biographer*. Literary criticism raised to this level, where it removes the cuticle of lies, self-deceit, self-flattery and the habit and illusion which threaten daily to grow over reality, becomes creative literature in its own right, and, as such, usually produces its weakest impression on a first reading. This is all the more true of *The Progress of a Biographer* since the writing is restrained in the interests of strict uncompromising exactitude, the style itself is tightly and carefully compressed, and the general tone uneuphuistic and unspectacularly reasonable and commonsense.

It is not the pure analytical brilliance alone which highlights this book as a supreme effort of the creative imagination; there is a sterling quality, too, about these final essays. For sustained achievement in this field of literature it is difficult to find a parallel. Although there is little aesthetic or impressionistic ornamentation, no romantic elaboration, and although the rule of economy is at all times rigidly applied so that no superfluous sentence was permitted to survive the first drafts, the tone is never too austere, too stern. The summary dogmas and verdicts of Johnsonian criticism which Kingsmill shared whenever his will was provoked more than his imagination was stimulated, are at last perfectly controlled. His natural aptitude for practical sense is employed less upon passing judgments than upon the interpretation of his individual and emotional response to literature. He did not aim at conveying the nature of his enjoyment as a reader, but at revealing the truth which lay at the root of a piece of writing, by relating it to his own experiences and to the individual character of its author. For his concentration was focussed unremittingly upon the unconscious personal impulse which he detected behind the formation of a creative work. None, too, of Kingsmill's vital and exuberant personality is readily discernible in these essays, unless it is that unusual mixture of humour and wit which Kenneth Hare, the poet, first discovered in him. Humour, sanity, erudition and insight are blended together within an overall simplicity, which excludes nothing of relevance.

The label stuck on Kingsmill as a writer, that of being an unoriginal debunking biographer, is peculiarly inaccurate, and dates back to 1928 when his *Matthew Arnold* appeared. "There was not a great deal, perhaps," one sentence of Kingsmill's obituary notice in *The Times* ran, "that was original in his style of biography, which derived from the uninhibited example of the early 1920's." It is ridiculous that all his works since that time should suffer under a totally inappropriate misconception and so naturally remain totally unappreciated. As the label in question comes off with little trouble, it is worthwhile attempting to remove it now, so that his writing may be judged in future without any vicariously pre-conceived prejudice.

Mr. J. I. M. Stewart, writing on biography in *The Craft of Letters in England* states that Kingsmill tried to improve on Lytton Strachey by touching up on people's absurdities, while in Mr. H. Sherard Vines's *A Hundred Years of English Literature* Kingsmill is aligned with the imitators of Lytton Strachey without comment. These are by no means the only books in which he is portrayed as a disciple of Strachey, and in yet another such work, Morton Daowen Zabel's *Craft and Character in Modern Fiction*, grouped together with two other writers with whom he had little in common, he is described

quite simply as "Stracheyan." This, then, has become the label
stamped on all his writing, and to call it initially in question
it is necessary only to point out that one of the two writers
with whom Kingsmill is grouped in this last work is C. E.
Bechhofer Roberts whose biographical novel on Dickens, *This
Side Idolatry*, is well known. It is doubtful whether either
author would be greatly delighted to find themselves thus
bracketed together, since Mr. Bechhofer Roberts once referred
to Kingsmill as "an amateur Dickensian masquerading as an
expert," although it appears that he had not read *The Sentimental Journey* at the time; and Kingsmill for his part suggested that the author of *This Side Idolatry*, owing to his
unorthodox partial dismissal of Dickens's affair with Ellen
Ternan, should bring out a revised version of his book under
the new title *This Side Adultery*.

Lytton Strachey considered that he modelled his biographical
technique on Johnson, and the difference between these two,
which Kingsmill elucidates in *The Progress of a Biographer*,
is in essence the difference between Strachey and Kingsmill
himself.

> "A mixture of severity and sympathy . . . reflects the
> combination in Johnson of a belief in absolute virtue and
> an equally strong realization of how far short of it even
> the best human beings fall . . . he was directed in every-
> thing he wrote by the saying of Jesus : 'None is good, save
> one, that is God.' Strachey, on the other hand, an epi-
> curean sceptic . . . wrote from the standpoint that no one
> at all is good, and that man's only rational occupation
> is to observe from a distance the contention of conflicting
> egotisms. . . . The difference in attitude between John-
> son and Strachey was therefore fundamental."

Although Strachey was far too intelligent to be taken in by
worldly hypocrisy and propaganda, he had not the temperament to immerse himself in reality. His *Eminent Victorians*,
written after the 1914-18 war during which he had been a

conscientious objector, is the work of a man looking at part of life from the outside. The horror of total war had driven him to become a spectator, and his detachment in *Eminent Victorians* often elongates into a remoteness which removed both himself and his subjects from any contact with real life and transmits them from human beings into mere puppets. Kingsmill's books, though for the most part tolerably impartial, are written from a personal standpoint, and his detachment, especially in his fiction, is sometimes shortened or abandoned altogether, causing him to lose his humour and to wobble uncertainly over into mawkishness. Strachey's weakness sprang from his apprehension of life; Kingsmill's from his intense longing for it.

As the memory of war grew dimmer in people's minds, Strachey gingerly approached life once more and began to take some part in it. But he so dramatized it as to create a buffer between him and the stark unromantic nightmare of reality which, if no longer in the limelight, still lurked, he felt, somewhere in the dark shadowy corners of the stage. The drama of history which he presented in his later books was shrunk down in fact to the dimensions of a stage play, and in the circumstances it is not with surprise that we learn he wished to become a dramatic poet. His *Elizabeth and Essex* indeed, as Francis Birrell has pointed out, is almost a sketch for a play. That he did not become a dramatist was due to his doubts concerning his own creative power, but had he done so, the theatre would surely have given rein to his worst qualities and his name would now have meant little more to us than that of Stephen Phillips. Kingsmill, on the other hand, wished to become a novelist and did not do so to any great extent due to other people's doubts regarding his capabilities in this direction. Whereas Strachey desired to elaborate more flamboyantly upon the inconsequence and colourful romance of life, Kingsmill wanted to penetrate more deeply the mysteries of life. That neither of them did so is a blessing for which posterity should be grateful.

If Strachey was reacting from the horror, mockery and senselessness of existence for which he felt himself hereditarily responsible, Kingsmill was in revolt against the Puritanism of his home which he believed acted as an obstacle to his self-development and contact with reality. Strachey found human actions to be pointless yet frequently diverting as viewed from a distance; Kingsmill considered them to be often misdirected, usually inadequate and also frequently diverting. Strachey was a secular rationalist, Kingsmill a mystic. Strachey concentrated on the relatively unimportant in order to divert his attention from unpleasantness and to safeguard himself from preoccupation over the immense complexity of life, and whereas Kingsmill most often dealt with reality, Strachey, all too often dealt with triviality. Kingsmill lacks some of Strachey's sparkle and much of his inventive faculty, dramatic power and genius for artistic organization yet there is far more fundamental truth and depth of meaning in his writing. On reading Kingsmill one is implicated oneself; on reading Strachey one is part of an audience.

22

The Burden Laid

EARLY IN 1948 KINGSMILL STARTED ON HIS LAST NOVEL, *Miserimus*, based on an inscription which he and Hesketh Pearson had found together in a West Country churchyard. But work on this was halted almost as soon as it had begun, when at the beginning of March, he was taken ill, spending a number of nights up with attacks of vomiting. He recovered for a few days, but another bout of illness followed which lasted some weeks and left him very weak physically, though mentally he felt first-rate. "I would like even more to be comfortable, sheltered, warm, mildly and delicately fed," he wrote to Hesketh Pearson, "Mozart in the distance; no work, no worries; no time or space; no infinity or eternity; no vitality, no absence of vitality."

At the end of March he had a haemorrhage and was moved to the Royal Sussex County Hospital in Brighton. The ambulance which was taking him to the hospital stopped first at the surgery of the doctor in charge of him, whose name, ironically enough, was Dickens. Here he was given a blood-transfusion with the help of the local vicar who, he noticed, at Dickens's suggestion wrapped a muffler round his neck so that the patient would not see that he was a parson and expect extreme unction to be forthwith administered.

Some twelve hours after his arrival at the hospital the principal medical officer, followed by a train of eager nurses came to visit him, and the following dialogue then developed.

P.M.O. "Well, you can wait a week if you like, to find out if you've got an ulcer."

H.K. "What'll happen at the end of the week?"

P.M.O. "You'll probably die."

H.K. "Any alternative suggestion?"

P.M.O. "You can be operated on at once to find out if you've got an ulcer."

H.K. "What'll happen in that case?"

P.M.O. "You'll probably die at once."

H.K. "A bit difficult to make up my mind especially in its present state. I'd like to discuss it with my wife."

P.M.O. "It's your decision. Not hers."

H.K. "Well, as there seems nothing in it, and I'd prefer drastic measures, I'll be operated on at once."

The operation was then carried out and no ulcer was found.* After this he began to recover quickly. On April 17 Malcolm Muggeridge visited him and noted in his diary that he was "in quite good shape, though of course somewhat haggard and old-looking. He was asleep when I got there, but when he woke up and saw me sitting by his bed such a smile of happiness came on to his face that I was deeply moved. We talked for two hours, and he was quite up to his old form. He is in a public ward, and quite the centre of interest to the other patients."

At the beginning of May he left hospital but again his progress on *Miserimus* was interrupted when he was commissioned to write an article for a well-known man's clothing establishment. "Dandies," as he called the piece gave him as much

* *Note:* For those susceptible to such information, Kingsmill's medical history may be summarized as follows. He was admitted to the Royal Sussex Hospital in Brighton on 30th March, 1948, suffering from haematemesis. A laparotomy was carried out, but no cause for his condition was ascertained. In the weeks that followed he gained in strength sufficiently to be released on 5th May, 1948. But during the next few months, while under the care of his own doctor, he had several more haemorrhages and attacks of vomiting and was readmitted to the Royal Sussex Hospital on 30 April, 1949. Here he was given a number of blood transfusions but remained too ill to be operated upon. After his death on 15th May, 1949, a *post mortem* was performed and a chronic duodenal ulcer found. The official cause of death was recorded as (i) haematemesis and (ii) a bleeding duodenal ulcer.

trouble as the most serious of his essays, but he was so short
of money that he could not refuse to do it. "One might easily
wax indignant," wrote Malcolm Muggeridge, "that penury
should have necessitated work of this kind when he might have
been getting on with, say, his book on Wordsworth. Such an
attitude would not be true to Hughie's memory. He laughed
over his 'Dandies' as heartily as he laughed over everything
else; took it neither more or less seriously than he took his other
labours. 'All the world in a grain of sand,' was one of his
favourite quotations from Blake. By the same token, all literature in his 'Dandies'."

The picture of Kingsmill as seldom able to cease from jovial
appreciation of his own poverty, drudgery and obscurity is far-
fetched. The man who ever since the age of eight had dreamed
of writing a work of literature that would last, to whom there
was no alternative to writing and whose mysticism even was
subject to the imagination, who found calmness in moments
of physical danger—on the mountains and during the war—
in his conviction that there was unique work for him to do, is
unlikely to have been convulsed with merriment at having to
rise to labours which drained his energy without furthering his
ambition. That he might make fun of "Dandies" in the company of friends is scarcely conclusive proof of his inner content-
ment. It is a popular fallacy to believe that humour implies a
lack of seriousness, whereas it merely indicates an absence
of earnestness—a very different thing. On its highest level
"where it is impersonal and disinterested," Kingsmill believed
humour to be "an illumination of reality not a refuge from it."
And the reality of his own life, often depressed him when his
humour and vitality were in abeyance.

While engaged in writing "Dandies" he took to his bed,
became very feeble and had to be confined to "sickly slops of
which I am heartily weary." He was suffering, he said, from
"fatigue and general fed-up-ness, stimulated on this occasion by
all this 'Dandies' business. One doesn't literally stomach this
kind of thing well at my age."

Instancing Kingsmill's introductory memoir to Leonard Dobbs's *Shakespeare Revealed* as an illustration, Malcolm Muggeridge has given the opinion that "perhaps he wrote best when he was least painstaking." There is indeed a naturalness and a charm in this memoir, but it is not through this or through "Dandies" that Kingsmill's name will live. On the other hand its composition took up so much of his time and trouble, that he wrote to Dobbs's executors to apologize for the delay. Of all his books, with the exception of *The Casanova Fable*, *Matthew Arnold* took least time to complete—even less than *The Sentimental Journey*—and was the least painstaking and the least satisfactory of all his biographies. The *Frank Harris* though, which Malcolm Muggeridge praised so enthusiastically, had germinated for many years within him and was composed with meticulous care.

Great care was also expended on *Miserimus*, of which he completed some fifteen thousand words. The two essential qualities which an author must exercise in writing a successful book are sympathy and detachment. *Miserimus*, like most of his fiction, contains some beautiful and arresting passages, but it also illustrates the basic flaw in nearly all his novels—his lack of detachment, amounting in places to overt sentimentality. Most vivid, once again, is the white-hot intensity of his longing for love and happiness, before which the rickety artificial barriers he erected in his own life are altogether dissolved, the dams of restraint are suddenly burst open and into the lake of unreality which appears, he pours his desire for financial security and his hope of a permanent state of happiness hereafter. The result is at times confused and almost absurd. A clear example of this is to be found in *Miserimus*, where Maurice Stirling, the Kingsmill-like hero, is out walking through the countryside with Enid Mitchell, a young girl with whom he is falling in love.

"Beneath them orchards and meadow land sloped down to the Severn Sea, and over the Welsh mountains on the further shore light sunny clouds were dissolving and forming again. On the way he talked about Wordsworth and Coleridge, and she listened to his voice. Leaving the high road, they went up for over a mile through ferny woods, and coming out into the open saw before them the flank of the majestic mansion where Wordsworth and his sister had lived on a rental of £23 a year. Facing its front there was a high steep slope on the ridge of which they sat down to recover their breath. 'Oh if life were always like this!' Enid murmured."

One must read this passage with care to ascertain whether Enid who, in the last two sentences, is merged with the character of Maurice, and who speaks for him, is referring to their present feelings of serenity, or to the value of unfurnished property, *circa* 1800.

Miserimus shows all the signs of having been written with an impaired vitality. The tone is subdued and melancholy, as if everything is seen through a grey film. His weary impatience with routine is very clearly shown in *Miserimus*, for although there are passages which are compressed, there are other places where half a page or more is devoted to nothing much more than a few people congratulating each other on the fine weather. Whereas in his earlier long novels he was inclined to skip everyday routine, in *Miserimus* he seems to bow his head and accept it into the book. The result is that some pages make dull and uninspired reading.

Written in bad health, after emerging from one hospital and before entering another, this fragment is a tragic document. The text itself seems to hold little genuine inspiration, and gives the impression that Kingsmill sat down one day to a blank piece of paper and started to write almost the first idea which came to mind for no other reason than that a publisher had at long last agreed to take another novel from him. The writing is as well and carefully phrased as ever and just as clear, yet the total effect seems uneven and almost jerky.

But it was impossible for Kingsmill to write something that was wholly uninspired, and sometimes his old enthusiasm momentarily quickened and he brought in images which shone like tiny jewels set in a background of grey paste. It is as if the sun glimmers suddenly down through a dull and bleary winter day to light up the world for a few moments with colour and life.

During these weeks Kingsmill was also engaged in writing his last poem. This poem was still incomplete at the time of his death, and was given no name. It is written in the same metre as *Night and Morning*, and he again uses the third person.

The poem opens with the picture of a man walking along a mountain track, the air soft about him, the sky luminous above. He does not know why he is there nor from where he has come, but he is unquestioning and content.

> "He has forgotten all, the journey's start
>   Along a sunken valley in deep shade,
>   The gorge whose dreadful torrent drained his heart
>   And the dark wood where he was most afraid."

The poem goes on to describe the progress of this journey. The darkness of the wood had dissolved and the traveller's fear changed to expectation as his eyes gazed over the plain beyond.

> "Grey meadows and still streams and branches clear
>   Against the deepening dawn, and far away
>   Closing the plain, a high-hung mountain where
>   Upon its upper slopes, faint sunshine lay."

With these lines, giving the infinite hope of youth, the first verse closes. The second and last verse develops the theme by showing how the beauty of dawn changes to the blistering and weary heat of day, the unceasing disillusion of the adult over past dreams, and expectations and desires. The scene opens in an old city, mellow and beautiful in the gathering light. At

first the early promise of the first verse looks like being fulfilled. There is a stir of happiness about the streets, but soon
a strangeness overclouds the city and descends heavily upon its
people and on "his own heart, too." The first certainties fade
and give way to confusion, and happiness and the feeling
of immortality are worn away to a vague echo.

> "A sense of something lost or not yet found
> Of something ended or not yet begun
> Driving him with the others round and round
> Through the close streets beneath the burning sun."

A third verse in which the heat and torment of the day
subside into the calm and serenity of evening and the stars
appear in the firmament above—minute points of gleaming
light not visible through the intense light of day—might well
have ended the poem. This would have completed the cycle,
from childhood to age, from intimations of immortality through
fear and the daily toils and tribulations of the world, back to a
release into forgetfulness and the reconciliation of acceptance
attained by the man on the mountain track at the start of the
first verse, who "walked, nor wondered whence he came, nor
why."

This poem shares the same beauty and the shortcomings
of *Night and Morning*. The unrelieved and unvaried beat of
the metre soothes one as a lullaby, and never gives one the impression, as in places it should, of waking into life. Kingsmill
would have been well advised to alter the metre to a shorter
number of syllables at various junctures, and so inject more
vitality and intensity into the poem.

But the energy which this poem lacks, no longer lay within
him. In August of this year, 1948, he was in bed with a severe
cold and sore throat. In November he experienced several
more bouts of sickness and had another slight haemorrhage.
During December he was again in bed, feeling very weak. The
entries in Malcolm Muggeridge's diary show however that
between these spells of illness he was as good company as ever,

and his mind still as quick and active. One entry, for June 9, leaves a quaint but vivid picture of him after leaving the hospital. "Returned home late," the entry runs, "and found Hughie in his night-shirt, reading a book on Keats—a comical but delightful figure."

The following February he had yet another haemorrhage, and the doctor warned him that he must have complete rest, for if the haemorrhages were to continue, he would soon be dead. In April he again entered the Royal Sussex County Hospital, where he was almost kept alive solely by blood-transfusions until May 15. Although very feeble and often in great pain his spirit remained remarkably serene, and he maintained his wonderful humour to the end. For two weeks he "clung on to life like grim death," as one of the nurses put it, and by the beginning of May he seemed to be recovering. "I don't know what's up with me," he remarked, "except that I have very bloody nights and could furnish three not very heroic martyrs with enough stuff to qualify on. I hope, however, to be definitely on the mend." To Hesketh Pearson he wrote, "Balmy spring breezes are blowing in from the sea outside, and all past springs revive, but I hope that this decaying old husk will release me at not too long a date to recover all the beauty of those old days in some other form."

On May 4 Hesketh Pearson called at the hospital to see him. He was afraid of over-exciting him, but Kingsmill seized his hand as he sat down by the bed, and would not let it go. When they had been talking for about an hour the sister approached to say he must now rest, and Pearson rose to leave. "The dear fellow was crying as he recalled a day we had spent at Winchester when we were writing our last book together," Pearson wrote, " 'About three years since Winchester, isn't it? How well I remember the old walled garden and the chimes!' I too remembered how we had strolled in the garden after dinner . . . and listened to the church bells; and, perhaps because I was unable to speak, I seemed to hear the words we had then uttered:

" 'One of the reasons why they move me so much,' I had said, 'is that their sound is unchanging from age to age, and Chaucer and Lady Jane Grey and Shakespeare and dear old Anna Seward all heard those chimes just as we hear them, and they accompany one's own journey in the same unchanging way. One's tastes take different forms from year to year, but church bells are always the same.'

" 'And so,' he had continued, 'they both recall the transitory expectations of the past and, being unchanged themselves, promise something that does not pass away'."

Three days later Malcolm Muggeridge visited him and in the course of their conversation asked him what books he would like to have. He replied at once that he preferred the *Lives of the Poets* to any of Shakespeare, for Johnson, unlike Shakespeare, had succeeded in purging himself of the "rancour, rage, self-pity and the furies of the will," and had become greatly reconciled to his fate. The innate scepticism of his mind, unlike Johnson's, did not intensify the horrors of death, but helped to lessen its terrors, to relieve his regret and allay his distress. He could never read without a catch in his voice that deeply philosophical passage from *Rasselas* which now, more than ever, expressed his own predicament:

"My mind is burdened with no heavy crime, and therefore I compose myself to tranquillity; endeavour to abstract my thoughts from hopes and cares, which, though reason knows them to be vain, still try to keep their old possession of the heart; expect, with serene humility, that hour which nature cannot long delay; and hope to possess, in a better state, that happiness which here I could not find, and that virtue which here I have not attained."

But if any of Shakespeare's lines came back to him during these final days, they were no longer the voice of his own deepest agony and desire, the mirage of love beyond his exhausted reach:

"Thou art a soul in bliss; but I am bound
 Upon a wheel of fire, that mine own tears
 Do scald like molten lead."

but the mystical reconciliation and tranquillity which momentarily overcomes Lear's rage, lines which had never failed to
move him :

". . . Come, let's away to prison :
 We two alone will sing like birds i' the cage :
 When thou dost ask me blessing, I'll kneel down
 And ask of thee forgiveness : so we'll live,
 And pray, and sing, and tell old tales, and laugh
 At gilded butterflies, and hear poor rogues
 Talk of court news; and we'll talk with them too,—
 Who loses and who wins; who's in, who's out;—
 And take upon's the mystery of things,
 As if we were God's spies; and we'll wear out,
 In a wall'd prison, packs and sects of great ones,
 That ebb and flow by th' moon."

Or perhaps, as he lay thinking back over his life, he remembered, too, the soliloquy of Claudius which expressed the conflict which had raged in the depth of his soul through so many
years.

"O limèd soul, that, struggling to be free,
 Art more engaged."

When Malcolm Muggeridge saw him in the ward for the
last time and shortly before his death, there was something
Kingsmill kept trying to say. But he was unable to form his
words and, walking away from the hospital, Muggeridge
remembered "the extraordinary stimulation of his company,
the wonderful laughter all along the Embankment and up
into the Strand, the invariable pleasure of seeing him and
hearing his voice, the incomparable richness of his mind and

of his humour and of his affection—so many unforgettable things said, scarcely a book which does not evoke some memory of him, scarcely a street which will not now seem slightly desolate."

In a deeply moving obituary notice which appears in *The New English Review* Muggeridge wrote : "He saw human beings as imprisoned souls, who yet could look forward with confidence to an ultimate release, and could find in human love, and the earth's dear loveliness, and their memories of past happiness, the image of an enduring felicity to come."

On Good Friday evening he was in great pain, and later told his wife that the ward had suddenly become full of blazing light in the middle of which stood an enormous cross, and it had seemed, in a moment of horror, that all the pain of Christ was passing to him like a devouring flame.

Both his wife and his daughter Edmée were with him at the end. About midday he became unconscious and revived only for two brief intervals during both of which he was too weak to speak. Shortly before nine o'clock his breathing diminished and became so soft as to be barely discernible. A few minutes later he raised himself slightly and gave a deep sigh, his head sank back on the pillow, and the strain was over.

Epilogue

KINGSMILL'S LIFE MAY BE CONVENIENTLY DIVIDED INTO FOUR parts.

From his birth until about the age of thirteen the chief influence on him was exerted by a mother whose aim it was that her children should always be good rather than happy. It was against this early training that Kingsmill spent the rest of his life in revolt, for although he refuted entirely the philosophy of Puritanism, some of its teaching remained deeply ingrained within his nature. Though by temperament a happy person he nevertheless retained some vague but unquenchable impression that it was necessary to experience hell in this life in order to qualify for heaven in the next, which gave to his hours of abandon an air of revolt. His latent Puritanism also revealed itself in minor masochistic idiosyncrasies—his periodic fasting; cold baths in the early morning; occasional runs through the countryside, suitably attired in shorts. Had his escape from Puritanism been more complete, his eager submission to any pretty girl who took his fancy would not have been so desperate, his yearning for love so intense. The inner conflict between his natural temperament and the ingrained Puritanism of his youth accounted, too, for his melancholy and his sentimentality, and was never fully resolved.

Part of the reason for his failure to overcome the influence of his mother on these first years lay in the partial misdirection of his energies. He considered that the most formative years of his life had not been the first twelve, but from the age of thirteen to twenty-two, when the dominant figure in his life had been his father. This was the period he remembered vividly as the most snobbish, diffident and self-contemptuous of his life. This substitution of the first period by the second, of his mother by his father, as the most formative influence on his character was due to a mixture of fear, tricks of memory, and the fact that such an alteration was more flattering to himself. The main deteriorating effects of this second period, lack of confidence and snobbery, were successfully eliminated later in life, unlike those emanating from his childhood. From this misconception, with its basic over-simplification of his own problems of self-development, sprang his occasional lack of sympathy with a biographical subject who had failed to free himself of his parents' stronger influence. Matthew Arnold is treated in this way in his attempted but unsuccessful revolt against his father, and, to a somewhat lesser degree, D. H. Lawrence, on failing to escape from the suppression of his mother.

The third period of Kingsmill's life may be said to have lasted until his break with the family business in 1927. The years as a prisoner of war with their unnatural restraint widened the conflict within him and deepened his melancholy. During this period he wrote three novels. *The Will to Love* sold four hundred and fifty copies, and *The Dawn's Delay* less than half that number, which necessitated him paying some fifty pounds to the publisher to whom he had guaranteed a sale of not less than two hundred and fifty copies. Anxious not to add fresh fuel to the fire of hostility which his wife was fanning against his literary pursuits, or to depress further the low opinions which the remainder of his family held of him he kept from them all information concerning his poor sales.

The comparative strength of his mother's power to that of his father is most strikingly demonstrated during the years 1920 to 1927. The lack of self-confidence which his father had injected into him, was kept in circulation by the poor reception of his first books, and persisted within him as a general but not intense sense of failure. He trained himself to depend on no one at all for support, and though he passionately desired encouragement he felt that, tired though he was of "giving out and getting nothing back," he could dispense with it if absolutely necessary.

His emotionalism, on the other hand, arose from the partial but not complete reaction against the shadowy but majestic figure of his mother. But whereas he found that he was able to endure years without recognition in company with those who disapproved of him, for a conveniently large sum of money, his love-affair in Switzerland coupled with his unsuccessful marriage blew such financial considerations to the winds and was directly responsible for his leaving his father's firm. Since the age of twenty-two he had restored sufficient confidence in himself to believe in his ultimate success. "As far as I am concerned," he said after a few years in the family business, "I would not change my life for any other form of existence, except possibly a private income."

His eventual decision to do so in 1927 must be attributed to those qualities which were developed within him as a result of the lasting power of his mother. Not only did his dramatic emotional intensity spring as a violent struggling reaction from Lady Lunn, but his marital relationship was an unconscious reproduction of his earlier feelings and attitude towards her.

The fourth and last period of his life extends from 1927 until his death. The continued neglect and ceaseless work of these years fed the sense of failure which his father had initially planted, and almost unrelieved penury gave it a new shape. This last disappointment, together with his great disappointment in love became interwoven and were symbolized for him by the girl in Switzerland who, in 1927, had rejected him in favour of someone more wealthy than himself.

Men who harbour strong feelings of disappointment are liable to be ruled in their judgments by personal prejudice. To guard against this, Kingsmill took immense pains in his compositions, rejecting anything which seemed too highly charged by his raw emotions or to have issued too directly from his own predicament. Quick writing is usually pure autobiography in someone not gifted with great powers of spontaneous invention, and is consequently biased to some extent unless first modified by considerable forethought. Kingsmill distilled his own experience through his writings, passing it through the fine comb of his intelligence and producing a prose, strong, sparkling and clear, free from all sediment. There is no cloudy stirring about in his works after uncertain meaning or flimsy sequence. The concoction has been perfectly decanted and prepared, and its purity will appear translucent weakness only to those who glance at it quickly and from a distance. The unhallowed divisions in his nature, whose direct offspring were sentimentality and aesthetic corruption, when integrated, could produce a prose that is permeated with freshness, delicacy and vitality.

The meticulous and circumspect care which went into his writing was the most perfect technique for literary criticism and, to a lesser degree, biography. Here he seldom obtruded himself too forcibly, but supported whatever he wrote by his strong and personal sense of reality, so that even his occasional excesses are often more instructive than the carefully reasoned passages of less able writers. The most successful of these books, his *Frank Harris, Samuel Johnson, The Return of William Shakespeare* and *The Progress of a Biographer,* all convey with wonderful clarity and directness his unique powers of imagination and insight, his integrity, his humour and the subtlety of his mind, the whole embellished by his wit.

But as applied to his fiction this technique of caution and wariness was disastrous, throttling him every time he essayed to give poetic expression to his deepest emotions. Between the lines of his novels the central conflict of his life is surreptitiously played out. The uneasy and familiar pattern repeats itself again and again; his emotions suddenly shoot surging past their straining barriers, are held quivering for one isolated moment, plunge cascading down into sentimentality and are finally sucked frothing back behind the dams of his self-restraint. But in one work of fiction, *The Dawn's Delay,* written

soon after being released from captivity in Germany, his vitality
and exuberance remained buoyant enough to sustain him
through a shorter course; he sees himself from the outside, his
yearning spirit is composed for a while, and he counsels resignation : "My friends, be patient."

THE END

Index

225